Journey of Faith

*A Guide for Beginning
and
Continuing Your Pilgrimage*

Rev. Dr. Morris Pepper

Rev. Dr. Robert S. Wood

Discipleship Ministry Team (CPC)

Memphis, Tennessee 2015

©2015 by the Cumberland Presbyterian Church. Prepared and published by the Discipleship Ministry Team of the Ministry Council of the Cumberland Presbyterian Church.

All Rights Reserved. No part of this book may be reproduced or transmitted in any form or by any means, electronic or mechanical, including photocopying, recording, or by any information storage or retrieval system, without permission in writing from the publisher. For information address Discipleship Ministry Team, Cumberland Presbyterian Center, 8207 Traditional Place, Cordova (Memphis), Tennessee, 38016-7414.

Funded, in part, by your contributions to Our United Outreach.

This book was originally published in 1985. A replacement publication is under development by the Discipleship Ministry Team. This edition is provided so that churches might make use of the pertinent information with the understanding that some materials are dated and no longer reflect the status of the Cumberland Presbyterian Church or the Cumberland Presbyterian Church in America.

Second printing March 2015.

ISBN-13: 978-0692406182
ISBN-10: 0692406182

OUR UNITED OUTREACH
Made Possible In Part By Your Tithe To Our United Outreach

TABLE OF CONTENTS

I. Beginning Where You Are 7

II. The Living Congregation 15

III. The Beginning and Growth of the Cumberland Presbyterian Denomination (1810-1883) 22

IV. The Growth and Renewal of the Cumberland Presbyterian Denomination (1883-Today) 27

V. The History and Mission of the Second Cumberland Presbyterian Church 37

VI. Our Relation to Other Denominations 46

VII. The Bible 53

VIII. Christian Worship 62

IX. The Sacrament of Baptism 70

X. The Sacrament of the Lord's Supper 78

XI. Living As A Christian 85

XII. Our Commitment 93

XIII. Christian Growth 101

To the Reader

This book is a guide for learning more about what it means to be a Christian and a church member.

It is to be used by those who are enrolled in a class on the subject.

It is to be read by the student.

You will be joining in a Journey of Faith with other people. You may wish to think of yourselves as pilgrims. Pilgrims are seekers. They are on the way toward knowledge of God. They travel an unending road of Christian growth.

In order to get the most out of this book, follow the suggestions in it for further reading. This reading will be done largely in the Bible. Be sure, too, to do the activities planned for you.

Take your time in reading. Don't rush. Ask questions and share thoughts with the people reading it with you.

You are on a journey. Keep a log of it. A log is any record of progress, as on a journey, any kind of journey. A log is kept by the captain of a ship. The log has a record of the speed of the ship, its progress, its position, and any unusual events. A log is kept by the captain or pilot of an aircraft. A record of the speed, flying time, experiences, and history of the craft is made. So, why not keep a log for your Journey of Faith? Directions for making entries will be given in the various chapters. Use a notebook that will be of lasting quality.

Morris Pepper

Robert S. Wood

A Greeting from the Writers

Welcome to the Journey of Faith. We will not be flying or riding in an automobile. We will not walk. We will travel by imagination. We will travel in mind and spirit. On our journey of faith, we have to take every step on our own.

We have written this book with love and care. We have looked forward to meeting you in mind and spirit. We will enjoy going part of the way with you on your journey of faith.

We pray God will go with us together. We trust God will cause us to grow in faith and life as long as we live.

Morris Pepper
Robert S. Wood

CHAPTER I
Beginning Where You Are

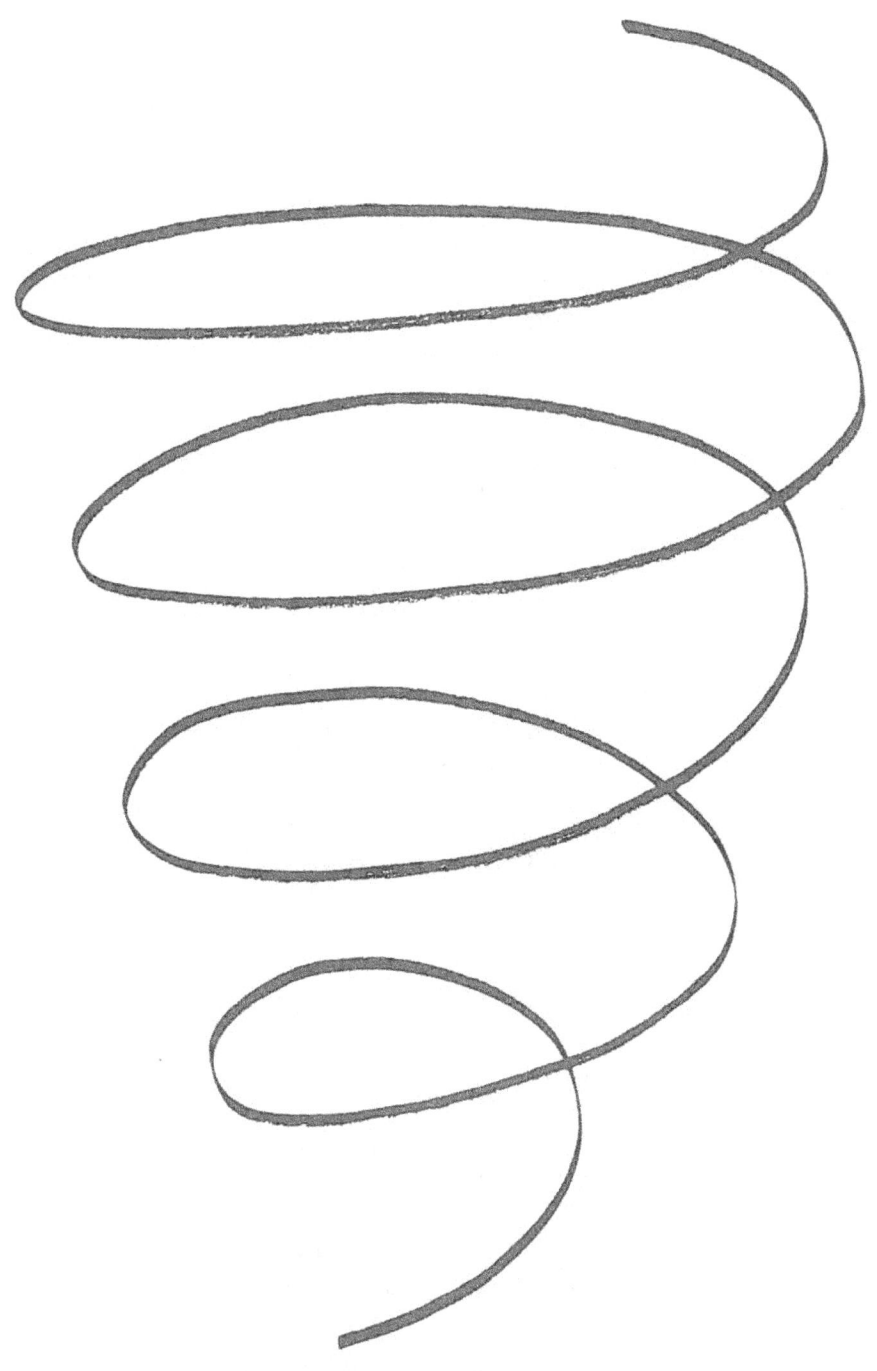

The spiral is the symbol of our journey of faith. It moves upward to higher levels and outward to more life all the time.

Beginning Where You Are

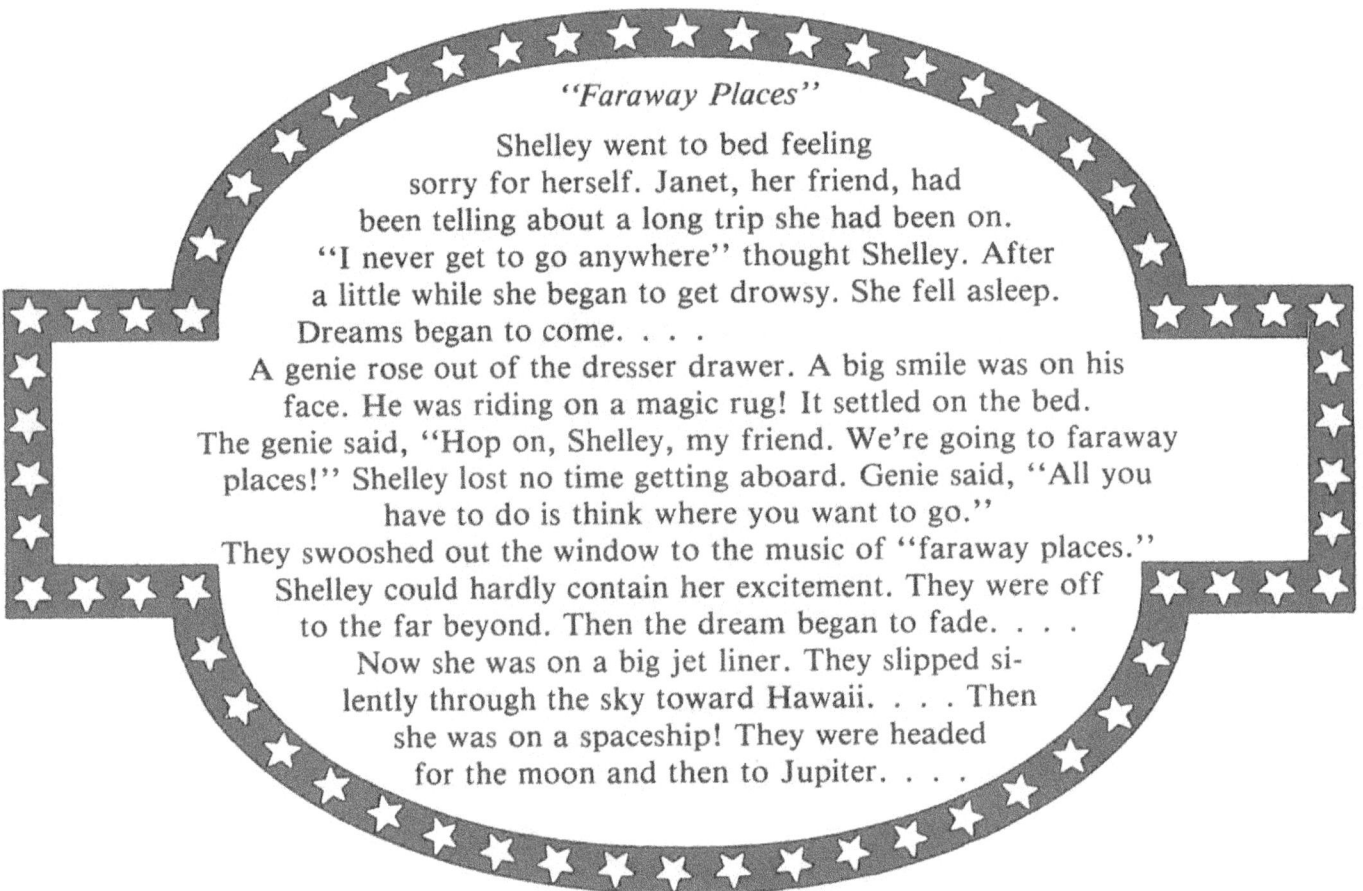

"Faraway Places"

Shelley went to bed feeling sorry for herself. Janet, her friend, had been telling about a long trip she had been on. "I never get to go anywhere" thought Shelley. After a little while she began to get drowsy. She fell asleep. Dreams began to come. . . .

A genie rose out of the dresser drawer. A big smile was on his face. He was riding on a magic rug! It settled on the bed. The genie said, "Hop on, Shelley, my friend. We're going to faraway places!" Shelley lost no time getting aboard. Genie said, "All you have to do is think where you want to go."

They swooshed out the window to the music of "faraway places." Shelley could hardly contain her excitement. They were off to the far beyond. Then the dream began to fade. . . .

Now she was on a big jet liner. They slipped silently through the sky toward Hawaii. . . . Then she was on a spaceship! They were headed for the moon and then to Jupiter. . . .

You're on a Journey

"Faraway Places!" We all like to go on trips. Journeys. Travels. We like to see new places and faces.

Well, you are on a journey. Not through space, not on a rug or a jet, but you are on a good and wonderful journey. It is the journey of life. You began it when you were born. You have gone places and seen things since then. Think of all you have learned . . . and you have hardly begun. There is no way of knowing where the journey of life will take you. What a gift!

A Journey of Faith

You are also on another kind of journey. It is a journey of faith. Abraham was one of the first ever to take such a journey. The Old Testament tells that he left Haran to go with his family to the Promised Land. He went out not knowing where he was going. But God sent him and went with him. (Read Genesis 12:1-5)

On a journey of faith you travel in trust. You don't know where the end will be. In fact there will be no end. It is the going, the traveling, the seeing, the learning that matters. You trust God to go with you. You don't ask God to look out for you. You believe God will. Like Abraham, you travel by faith.

On a journey of faith you learn about God. You ask who and what God is; what God has done; how God works. You ask questions. You never stop asking. You try to find answers.

On a journey of faith you go and see for yourself. You don't ask someone to tell you about it. You explore. You ask: What is true? What is right? What is real? What can I believe? What is life all about? What does it mean to be alive? How does God fit into my life? Who was Jesus? What is the Holy Spirit? Where did the Bible come from? What is the church? There seem to be more questions than answers. On a journey of faith you live with questions—and faith. You trust what you cannot know.

You have been on this journey now for some time. You began it when you were born. You have made some discoveries. You have come to believe some things. You have come to know something of what it means to be Christian. You have traveled with others, mainly members of your family and church. Your faith has been shaped by them. You inherited beliefs. You take them for granted. You probably never question them. They are a part of your life.

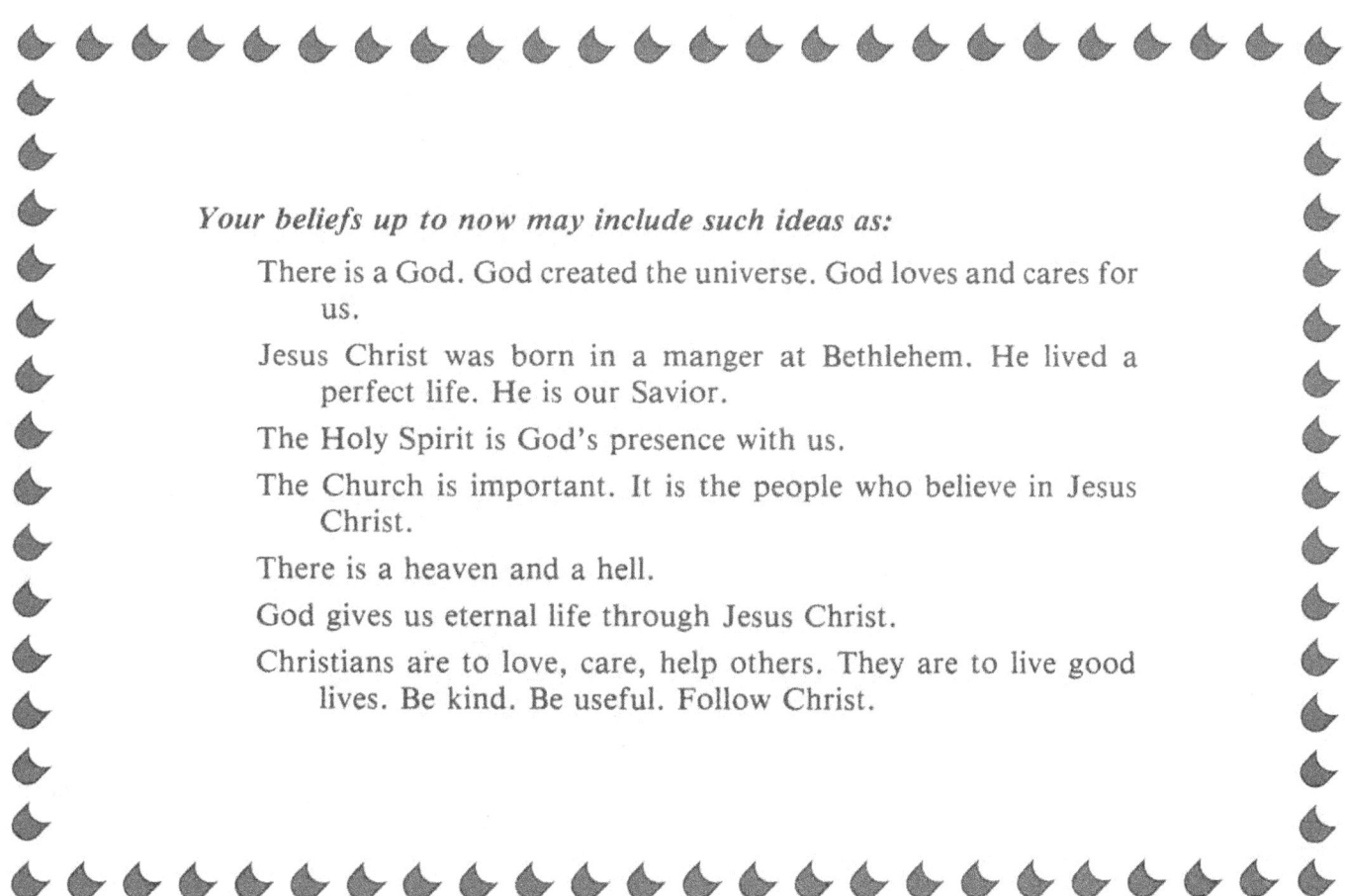

Your beliefs up to now may include such ideas as:

There is a God. God created the universe. God loves and cares for us.

Jesus Christ was born in a manger at Bethlehem. He lived a perfect life. He is our Savior.

The Holy Spirit is God's presence with us.

The Church is important. It is the people who believe in Jesus Christ.

There is a heaven and a hell.

God gives us eternal life through Jesus Christ.

Christians are to love, care, help others. They are to live good lives. Be kind. Be useful. Follow Christ.

You have a decision to make. Will you continue this journey of faith on your own? Once begun it never ends. Faith develops gradually, step by step. You do not get it all at once. Your beliefs are developed one by one. They change from time to time. There will never come a time that you are not on this road of faith. You will want to know and obey God better and better as time passes. It gets more interesting the further you go.

Now may be the time for you to think more about your inherited faith and to consider making it truly your own. And to make it greater. (Read Philippians 3:12-14.) You will have many years ahead to develop a strong faith. The following paragraphs give some stages through which you will go if you make a new beginning on the journey.

Shaping your faith requires Experiencing . . . Sorting Out . . . Choosing . . . and Practicing. These milestones may not come in the order named, but they are all important.

Experiencing

Experiencing faith means having religious feelings. No one can have these feelings for you. No one can have them and pass them on to you. You have to do your own experiencing.

These religious feelings may include:

    Wonder at God's love
    Inner warmth from God's presence
    Joy and thanksgiving for God's gifts
    Love when you think of Jesus Christ
    Relief when you are forgiven
    Longing to be a better person
    A desire to become a Christian
    A sense of being led by God's Spirit

Look this list over again. Have you ever had any of these feelings? To what degree? Under what conditions? In what situations? Take time to think. Remember that everyone does not have the same feelings. Some feel one way and others feel a different way. Some feel more than others and some less.

These feelings come at different times and places. Check the times and places you have had some of them.

_____ At worship in church
_____ During camp
_____ Out in nature
_____ Alone at a quiet time
_____ While reading a book
_____ While viewing a film
_____ While singing at church or in a group
_____ When helping someone
_____ While talking to someone about God

_____ _____
_____ _____

You may not have had any of these feelings. Your faith may be largely one you have accepted from someone else. You may agree to it and live by it. But it is hardly your own because you have not experienced it. Without experiencing, you will not make faith your own.

This is all right if it is where you are. Don't rush yourself. Don't try to have feelings which are not real to you. Give yourself time. Keep on reading and studying about faith. Learn as much as you can. In time you will begin to have religious feelings on your own. We believe that God comes to each person. When God does come to you, you can make your own response.

You may have had some experiences like those mentioned above. You may not have felt strongly. You may not understand much about them. That is all right. Don't be afraid. Don't get in a hurry. Let life happen to you. Keep open. As you continue to grow and develop more will come to you. You are on your way toward making faith your own.

Religious feelings can be very stirring and strong. Or they may be very gentle. Some people will be so touched that they will shed tears. Others will not. Some will be able to talk about what is happening to them. They may show joy and appear to be very happy. Some will not. Either way is all right.

The depth of feeling will depend to a great degree on your nature. Some people are very excitable. Other are quiet. Some are talkative, and others say little. Don't worry about feelings. Let them be what they naturally are for you. If you want to talk about them, that is good. If not, that is all right too.

You can expect to have religious experiences when you are ready. Don't let other people rush you. Some who do not understand faith and life may try to hurry you. They may try to scare you. Others may press you to decide because they think you ought to. Do not let these people influence your actions. Talk over your feelings with your parents, pastor, or someone with whom you feel comfortable. God can speak to you through them. God loves you and understands you. God knows how far along you are in your growth.

Sorting Out

To sort out means to separate according to kind. A basket may have different kinds of fruit in it. To sort them out means to put each kind of fruit together. Sorting out your faith is asking what you believe about different subjects. It can help you see where you are regarding your faith. Have you ever asked yourself: What do I really believe about God? Jesus Christ? The Church? The World? Myself?

Use the following checklist of beliefs to see how far along you are in your faith journey. Take time in marking it.

A Checklist: Where Am I in My Faith?

Given below are several statements of belief. They have to do with what you feel or believe about God, Jesus Christ, the Holy Spirit, and other subjects. They are only suggestions. We are not telling you what to believe. We are trying to help you find out for yourself what you believe.

Mark your response to these on a scale from 1 to 5. 1 is low, 5 is high. Note that some of the statements say "I believe" and others say "I feel." If you believe or feel strongly, mark 5. If you believe or feel very little, mark 1. If you believe or feel to some degree, mark 2, 3, or 4.

There are no wrong answers. Your answers mark where you are in your feelings or belief. You are O.K. where you are.

Where Am I in My Faith in God?

I feel that God loves me.	1	2	3	4	5
I feel that God forgives me when I ask.	1	2	3	4	5
I feel that God is in control of the world.	1	2	3	4	5

Where Am I in My Faith in Jesus Christ?

I believe that in Jesus Christ, God became a human being.	1	2	3	4	5
I believe that Jesus Christ died for my sins.	1	2	3	4	5
I believe that he rose from the grave.	1	2	3	4	5

Where Am I in My Faith in the Holy Spirit?

I feel that the Holy Spirit is God's presence with me.	1	2	3	4	5
I feel that the Holy Spirit guides me.	1	2	3	4	5
I feel that the Holy Spirit gives me strength in all needs.	1	2	3	4	5

Where Am I in My Faith in the Church?

I believe that the church is those who believe in Jesus Christ.	1	2	3	4	5
I feel that I need the church.	1	2	3	4	5
I believe that the church does good things for people.	1	2	3	4	5

Where Am I in My Faith in Eternal Life?

I believe that death is not the end of life.	1	2	3	4	5
I feel that eternal life is a relation with God that never ends.	1	2	3	4	5
I believe that eternal life is a gift from God through faith in Jesus Christ.	1	2	3	4	5

Where Am I in My Faith About the World?

I believe that God created the universe and the world.	1	2	3	4	5
I believe that the world is good.	1	2	3	4	5
I feel that I am to keep the world good and beautiful.	1	2	3	4	5

Where Am I in My Faith Concerning Myself?

I feel that God created me.	1	2	3	4	5
I believe that I am made in the image of God.	1	2	3	4	5
I feel that God gave me gifts of ability.	1	2	3	4	5
I feel that God wants me to use my gifts for others.	1	2	3	4	5
I feel good about myself.	1	2	3	4	5

Where Am I in My Faith in Prayer?

I believe that we are to pray.	1	2	3	4	5
I believe that prayer is more than asking; it is also thanking, praising, thinking about others, and waiting for God to guide our thoughts.	1	2	3	4	5
I feel that God hears our prayers.	1	2	3	4	5

(The above list is not complete. As you continue your faith journey, you will think of other statements of belief to examine.)

Take time now to ask yourself these questions:
  (1) Why did I respond as I did?
  (2) What was the most difficult question for me?
  (3) Where can I find help in sorting out my faith?
You may report your answers to your class.

Choosing

Choosing is also a part of shaping our faith. You decide for yourself what you will believe. As your experience of life becomes wider and deeper you will make more choices. In choosing there will be questioning. You will ask what you think is true and what is not. It is natural for you to ask questions about your faith.

Be as sure as you can that you are making the right choices. In arithmetic and science you can prove an answer or idea to be correct. You cannot prove a belief to be true in this way. For example, you cannot prove that God exists. You believe God is. You act on that belief. Testing beliefs by acting on them makes your faith stronger.

You make your own choices depending on your faith to guide you. You will use your Bible to direct you. Your church also guides you and teaches you.

Practicing

To practice your faith is to live by it. You believe certain things. Then you live by them. Your faith is never real until you live by it.

Examples of Living by Your Faith

(Put ✓ by two which you will especially try to practice.)

If you believe God forgives, then ask and receive forgiveness and live like a forgiven person. ____

If you believe God hears your prayer, pray. ____

If you believe God saves you through Jesus Christ, trust and commit yourself. ____

If you believe God leads you by the Holy Spirit, ask for guidance. ____

If you believe you are to forgive others, be forgiving. ____

If you believe you are to do good to others, do good to them. Live out your faith. Make it your own through action. Read James 2:14-17 and 1 John 3:18. ____

You are on a journey of faith. You are beginning where you are to think further about its meaning. There will be many more miles to go before it is completed. There is much more you need to learn. This book is written to help you.

Jargon for the Journey

Jargon is the words or language used in talking about particular subjects. There is a language (jargon) used in talking about the Christian religion. The following words (jargon) are defined so you will understand them as you use them.

BELIEF OR DOCTRINE: A belief or a doctrine is a statement of what we believe about God, Jesus Christ, the Holy Spirit, salvation, the church, Christian growth, and other religious subjects.

FAITH: Faith is trust and commitment. It is acting on what you say you believe. For example, if you believe Jesus Christ saves you, you trust him to do so.

CHURCH: The church is people. It is the people who answer God's call and say they believe in Jesus Christ as Lord and Savior.

LOG: Any record of progress, as on a journey. See the next section for reference to "Log for Journey of Faith."

Scriptures About Faith

If you want to find out more that the Bible says about faith, read the following passages:

> Hebrews 11:1-6
> James 2:14-17
> 1 John 5:4
> John 3:15, 16

Use the *Good News Bible (Today's English Verson)* and other translations. Compare them. After reading, rewrite them in your own words and record them in your book, "Log for Journey of Faith." How would you now define faith? Put the answer in your book.

A Question About the Symbol

After reading this chapter, do you think the spiral is a good symbol for your journey of faith? Why? Why not?

Faith Shaping, by Stephen D. Jones, Judson Press, Valley Forge, PA, 1980, was used as a resource for some of the ideas in this chapter.

CHAPTER II
The Living Congregation

"Come to the Lord, the living stones . . . Come as living stones, and let yourselves be used in building the spiritual temple."
1 Peter 2:4,5, Good News Bible

"Christ Jesus himself being the chief cornerstone."
Ephesians 2:20, RSV

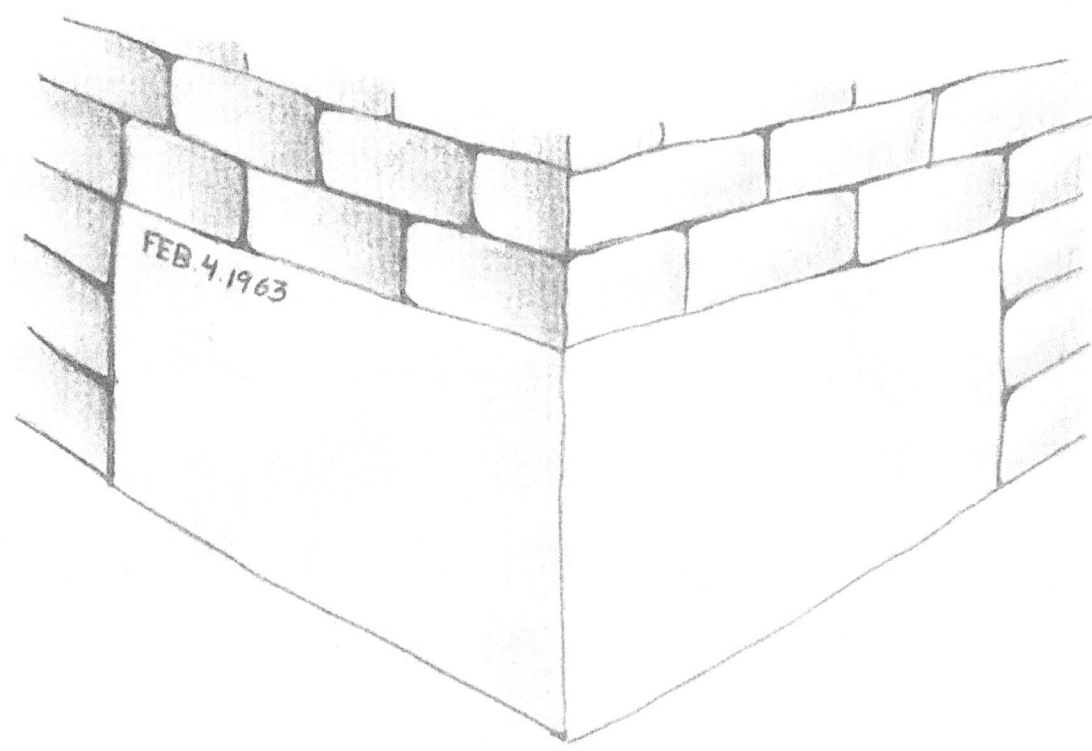

A cornerstone is a point of beginning for some buildings. In Bible times, the large stone was set into the ground and made level. On it and out from it other stones were laid to make the building. A building with a cornerstone stood firmly against time and storm.

Jesus Christ is the chief cornerstone for the church. Your congregation is part of this church built on faith in him.

The cornerstone is a good symbol for the church.

The Living Congregation

You are probably related in some way to a congregation of God's people. A congregation is a particular church made up of people who worship and serve together. Your family may belong. You may not be a committed member but may be thinking about becoming one.

The journey of faith is never taken alone. It is made in company with others. They include your family and congregation, as well as friends. This chapter will help you learn more about your congregation and its part in your Christian pilgrimage.

The Congregation Is a Living Community

The congregation is a living community made up of people in relation to God and each other. To congregate means to meet or gather together. The biblical background of the word suggests that we meet because God calls us together. God meets with us. The hour set for any church meeting to do its work may be thought of as an appointment with God.

Think of the many meetings of your congregation. Perhaps not a single week passes that members of your family do not meet with others in the church at least once.

You meet for worship to celebrate your faith. You meet in small groups for Sunday school and at other times. You meet for church meals in thanksgiving to God for blessings received and to share in each other's lives.

You meet for funerals to share in the sorrow of those who have lost someone by death. You meet for weddings to share in the joy of families who are uniting in marriage. You meet for special services, such as revivals, Christmas, Easter, and New Year's worship. Members of the congregation take part in the Cumberland Presbyterian Women and Men's Fellowship.

There is a mixing of people throughout the year as they plan and carry on the work of the church through the session, diaconate (board of deacons), and committees. Members join with other congregations in the community for union worship such as Thanksgiving.

These occasions make possible a growing knowledge of each other and a church family atmosphere. The people share so much of each other that they become a community.

The idea of a congregation and the church around the world as a community of people is expressed in the song, "We Are the Church."

16

We Are the Church

Words & Music by
Richard Avery & Donald Marsh

I am the church! You are the church! We are the church together! All who follow Jesus, All a-round the world! Yes, we're the church together.

1. The church is not a building, The church is not a steeple, The church is not a resting place, The church is a people.

2. We're many kinds of people
   With many kinds of faces,
   All colors and all ages, too, from
   All times and places. (Chorus)

3. Sometimes the church is marching,
   Sometimes it's bravely burning,
   Sometimes it's riding, sometimes hiding,
   Always it's learning: (Chorus)

4. And when the people gather
   There's singing and there's praying,
   There's laughing and there's crying sometimes,
   All of it saying: (Chorus)

5. At Pentecost some people
   Received the Holy Spirit
   And told the Good News through the world to
   All who would hear it. (Chorus)

6. I count if I am ninety,
   Or nine or just a baby;
   There's one thing I am sure about and
   I don't mean maybe: (Chorus)

Copyright © 1972 by Hope Publishing Co.
Carol Stream, IL 60188. Used by permission.

Learn to sing this song. It has an easy and happy tune. Ask your family to join with you. When your class meets, sing it together. What ideas of the church are expressed in it? The church as people? All kinds and ages of people? All who follow Jesus? People who share together? A people with good news? Others?

What kind of people are in your congregation? One kind or more? Does each person feel included? Are all people welcome? What are the ages of people in your church? Who is your oldest member? The youngest?

God's People Are Sinners

Although the church is made up of God's people, they are not angels. They are sinners. Sometimes they are hard to get along with. Sometimes they are stingy. Sometimes they are careless about attendance. Sometimes they will not work in the church. They fail to be their best.

At other times they are faithful in worship and service. They try to be helpful and to live in the spirit of Jesus Christ. They are getting stronger in the faith. However, they are not perfect in their belief and living. They try to be better but fall short.

In spite of these facts about all of us, if we accept Jesus Christ as Lord and Savior, God accepts us. We live as forgiven sinners in the church.

It is truly amazing that God has chosen sinful people to be in the church and to do its work. God's acceptance of us is something to be celebrated. We ought to be glad about it. As weak, proud, and limited as we are, God loves us and gives us a place in the church!

Members of the New Testament church were not perfect either. An example is a disagreement in the congregation at Corinth. Read 1 Corinthians 1:10-13; 3:1-4. Someone once said about western films, "They always kill the bad guys." Paul was not interested in killing, or kicking out, the "bad" people. He tried to help them grow and improve.

We are wrong in referring to people as good and bad. We are all sinners. In the church, we are saved by God's love. None is better or worse than others. We are all sinners seeking to grow in our Christian living.

Your Relation to the Congregation

Think further of the congregation and your relation to it. You are a part of this group who influence each other. Some have more influence than others. Everyone influences others to some degree. Can you think of persons in your congregation who have made your life better? List some names in your "Log for Journey of Faith."

You see some members at Sunday school. You may mix with them in conversation before and after worship. You may laugh and joke with them. You may talk with them about happenings in the community. You enjoy each other. However, sometimes you may misunderstand and be misunderstood.

You go to worship with others. You welcome new members as they join the group. You may attend youth meetings and parties and go on trips. You go to church meals. You associate with the minister and other leaders. At home you probably talk about the church and your family's relation to it. All of these relationships influence you. You are learning more than you may realize about life and faith.

If you grew up in the congregation or have been a part of it for some time, you probably feel at home there. You feel loved and accepted. If your congregation is small you may be able to call every member by name. You know much about families and individuals. They are a part of your life. If your congregation is larger, you still know much about some of the people in it. Stop here and see how many names of persons in the congregation you can remember.

Notes to a Newcomer

You may be somewhat new in the congregation. You may not know many of its members. How can you go about getting better acquainted?

Begin on your own. Don't wait for others to come to you. Some members are timid. They may be afraid of new people. They often do not know what to say to them. Introduce yourself.

Ask your family to get acquainted with other families that include people your age.

Try to relate to someone who seems to know everyone. He or she will introduce you to others.

Go to group meetings of people your age. Keep going back. Don't stop if others seem a little slow to accept you. Give them time. Teachers and leaders will help you.

Learn to know the pastor. The pastor will like it if you introduce yourself. He or she may have so many people to see it may be hard to seek you out.

Listen more than you talk. It is better to keep quiet and learn about the group by observing than to talk too much.

Don't try to impress others with what you have done or can do. Let them find it out slowly. If you have something, they'll discover it. If you brag too much, you will push them away from you.

Learning More About the Congregation

In spite of all you already know, there are other things you still need to learn about your congregation. It will be helpful to you to get this information together. Put it in the "Log." This information is to be about the members of the congregation and what they are doing for God and people together through the church. If you are new in the congregation, you need to learn all you can.

This project will help you understand better what will be expected of you as a member. It will also point to the ways for service the congregation offers.

To guide you, questions and suggested activities are given. Follow the instructions.

Learning Who You Are as a Congregation

1. What is the name of the congregation?
   Why was it selected? Does it have any special meanings?
2. Some things about the history and background of the congregation.
   a. Find pictures of church events and persons of the past, such as: pictures of Sunday school classes, youth groups, session, deacons, groundbreaking ceremonies, building programs, former pastors, important people from years past, picnics and other social occasions, special mission projects, missionaries, special work projects. This will show you what your congregation is doing and has done.

      Ask your parents to help you. They can share in some of this information. You may want to take some of this material to class and share it.

      If you are new in the congregation, you may work with another member of the group.
   b. Recall the event in the life of the congregation which has meant most to you since you have been a part of it.
   c. List the special things your congregation does every year. Some of these may be: a picnic, a service trip by a group, ways of celebrating Christmas, Easter, Pentecost, New Year's. Include also any special services in which you have had visiting speakers.
3. The government of the church.
   List the names of the elders.
   List the names of the deacons.
   List the names of the trustees.
   List the names of the ministers you have had since you have been a part of the congregation.
4. Organizations of the church.
   List the names of the church organizations, such as Sunday school, Cumberland Presbyterian Women, men's fellowship, and youth fellowship.
5. Church committees.
   List the names of the church committees. State in one sentence what each committee does. The committees may include Worship, Building and Grounds, Missions, Christian Education.

All you have done in this assignment is to be shared with your class. The class may wish to share some of it with the congregation or with an organization in the church.

The Symbol

Think about the cornerstone, the symbol for the living Congregation. Who do you think the cornerstone represents? Who do the other stones symbolize. Using some building blocks, construct a building with a cornerstone.

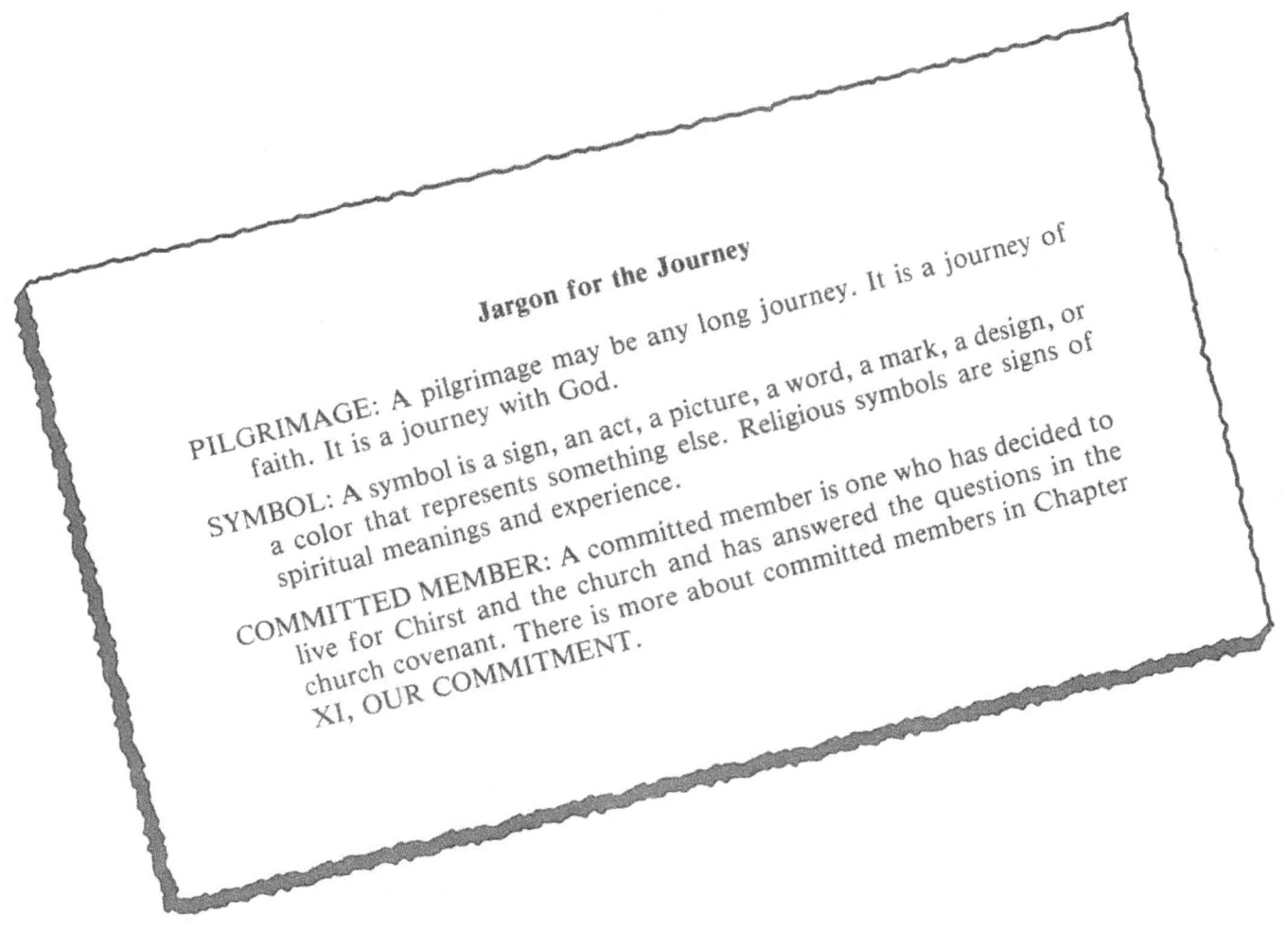

Jargon for the Journey

PILGRIMAGE: A pilgrimage may be any long journey. It is a journey of faith. It is a journey with God.

SYMBOL: A symbol is a sign, an act, a picture, a word, a mark, a design, or a color that represents something else. Religious symbols are signs of spiritual meanings and experience.

COMMITTED MEMBER: A committed member is one who has decided to live for Chirst and the church and has answered the questions in the church covenant. There is more about committed members in Chapter XI, OUR COMMITMENT.

"Learning Who You Are As a Congregation" was adapted from *Smaller Church Mission Study Guide*, by Henry Blunk (Philadelphia: The Geneva Press, 1978). Used by Permission.

CHAPTER III
The Beginning and Growth of the Cumberland Presbyterian Denomination
(1810-1883)

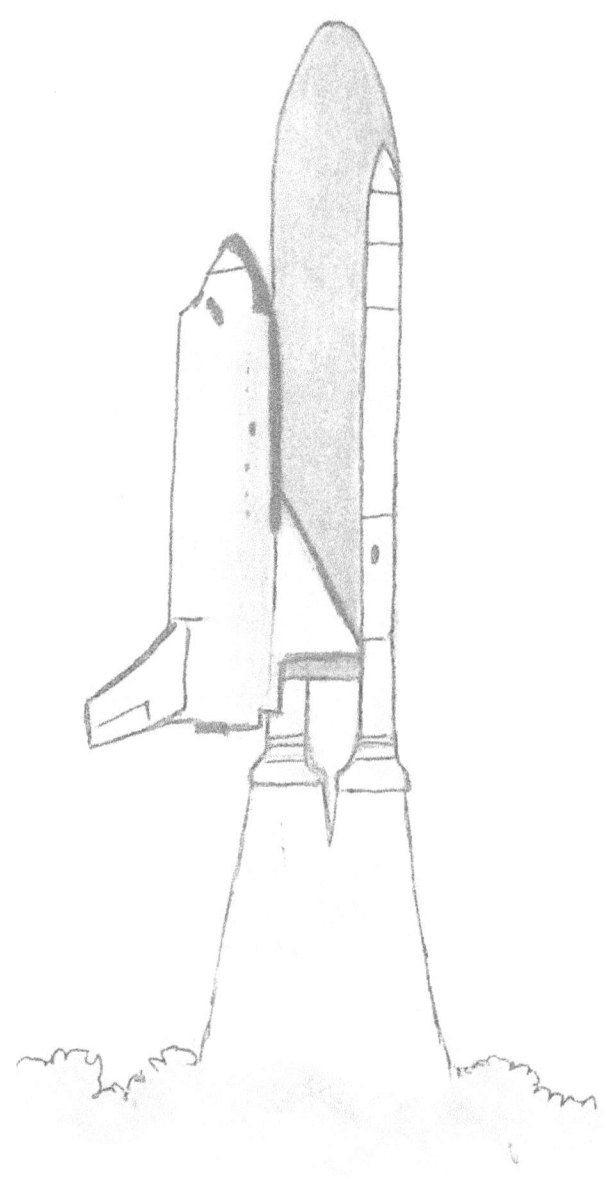

The rocket is a symbol of the new frontier in space. It is suitable for our denominations which were born on the early American frontier. Our churches serve on new frontiers today.

The Beginning and Growth of the Cumberland Presbyterian Denomination
(1810-1883)

Who Are We?

Henry and his father had gone to church early. Shortly after their arrival, a stranger drove up and got out of his car. He was looking for a church building.

He asked, "Can you tell me where the Presbyterian Church is located? I'm new here and don't know the town very well."

Henry's father replied, "I guess you are looking for Westminster. It is a Presbyterian congregation. You will find it at the intersection of Willow and Jefferson."

The man thanked him very cordially and left.

Henry was puzzled. He asked his father, "Aren't we Presbyterian, too?"

"Yes," he answered. "We are Cumberland Presbyterian."

Henry wanted to know more. They got into a question and answer conversation.

Some of the questions Henry asked were:
  How is the Cumberland Presbyterian Church different from other Presbyterian denominations?
  Where did the word Cumberland come from?
  When was the Cumberland Presbyterian Church organized? Where? Why?
  Is there anything special about it?
  What relation does it have to other Presbyterian denominations?
  Are their beliefs the same?

Perhaps you have asked some of the same questions. If so, this chapter will help you find some answers.

Our Roots

The Cumberland Presbyterian Church began on the American frontier in 1810. The first part of its name came from the Cumberland region of Kentucky and Tennessee where it was born. This area was in the south central part of Kentucky and the north central part of Tennessee. The second part of its name came from its roots in the Presbyterian Church.

The earliest beginnings of the Presbyterian Church were in Europe. John Calvin organized the first Presbyterian Church in Geneva, Switzerland, in 1536. The word Presbyterian comes from a Greek word meaning elder. It is a church governed by elders—teaching elders or ordained ministers and ruling elders, lay people chosen by the congregation.

As time passed people from Europe began to migrate to America. The majority of Presbyterians who came were Scotch-Irish. Francis MaKemie was one of the earliest Presbyterian ministers to come to America.

In 1706 a presbytery, the first one in this country, was organized in the city of Philadelphia. The Presbyterian Church grew rapidly and had great influence. John Witherspoon, a Presbyterian minister, was one of the signers of the Declaration of Independence.

The Western Movement

After the Revolutionary War a great western migration began. People pushed across the Allegheny Mountains and settled in Ohio, Kentucky, Tennessee, and other areas in the West and South. The church went with them. As the population grew, churches, including the Presbyterian, were organized.

The people on the frontier were not very religious. Only about one out of ten was a church member. The majority denied belief in Jesus Christ. Material things held their attention. They were concerned with survival—finding land, building homes, and making a living.

The Revival of 1800

A religious awakening began. It was called the Revival of 1800. James McGready, a Presbyterian minister from North Carolina, went to Kentucky. He became pastor of the Red River congregation in the Green River country. He stirred people up to great interest in the revival movement. It spread rapidly.

A number of ministers joined in the spiritual awakening. They preached sermons which stressed the need for salvation. They aroused the emotions of the people. They urged those who came to church to read the Bible, to pray and meditate. The people were urged to consider seriously their spiritual condition. Attendance at religious services grew as interest and concern for salvation became strong.

These revival services began in church buildings. Later outdoor camp meetings were started as a new way of reaching more people. Settlers came from miles around to meeting places, usually near a spring or stream. They camped out in the open. Services were held outside or under brush arbors. Ministers took turns in preaching and leading the people in prayer. Each meeting continued over several days at a time. The revival caught on with the people and it became a popular pastime.

Conflict Over the Revival

Strong opposition to the new methods of evangelizing arose. This conflict centered in Cumberland Presbytery of Kentucky Synod of the Presbyterian Church. The happenings there led to the birth of the Cumberland Presbyterian denomination.

Ministers in the presbytery became divided into two groups of five each—the Revival Party and the Anti-Revival Party. The Anti-Revival Party continued to believe, preach, and work as in the past. They fought the new attitudes, practices, and methods of the revival. Any change from what had been taught and practiced was opposed.

The Revival Party was made up of a group of mostly younger ministers. Some, though older in age, had only recently become ministers. They were open to change. They were strongly for the revival. They held meetings and preached evangelistic sermons.

They called for repentance, faith, and conversion. Everything possible was done to reach more people.

These ministers organized new churches and rode circuits. A circuit was an arrangement made to reach more people with the gospel. Churches, "societies" (fellowship groups), and communities were listed in a way to form a circle or round covering many miles throughout the country. Services were scheduled for every day. It often took weeks to reach all places in the circuit. After a short rest the ministers would start all over again or make the round of another area. The work was hard. They rode horseback through all kinds of weather in the rough wilderness country. This use of the circuit was necessary because there were not yet enough ministers to serve each church or settlement.

The dedication of these unusual people was due in part to the change in their beliefs and their new religious experiences. They rejected the old doctrine which taught that a set number of people was selected by God to be saved while others were to be lost. Their positive beliefs were:

Christ died for all people, not just part of them.
God called every person to be saved.
Whosoever believed in Jesus Christ was saved.
All babies dying in infancy were saved.
Being born again spiritually was necessary to become a Christian.
All who accepted Christ would be saved to eternal life.
Christianity was a religion of the heart. It was something to be felt as well as believed and lived. One could experience the presence of Christ who came into one's heart as one became a Christian.

All this was different from the religion they had been taught. It fitted into the kind of life they lived on the frontier.

Differences Over Ordination Rules

Another point of difference was the rule for ordaining men to be ministers. The Presbyterian Church had always insisted on the need for educated ministers. It required a knowledge of the Greek, Latin, and Hebrew languages and literature before ordination. This kind of education was available only in schools east of the Allegheny Mountains.

Members of the Revival Party rejected this rule. They were for educated ministers. But the situation called for more ministers as quickly as possible. The population and the church were growing rapidly. There was not time enough for men to go back east for an education. The Revival Party believed rules could be changed to meet the need without giving up good standards for education. The church could accept men who had ability and a sound faith and give them a good practical education. They could be ordained as ministers and serve well.

These differences about education of ministers were never settled. The argument kept going.

Cumberland Presbytery Broken Up

The conflict became so strong that some breakup seemed sure to happen. The Revival Party was now fewer in number than the Anti-Revival Party. The majority in Kentucky Synod held to old beliefs and practices. They backed the Anti-Revival Party. When it was voted that Cumberland Presbytery be broken up to defeat the Revival Party, Kentucky Synod agreed. This left the members of the Revival Party with no presbytery. They were now outside.

They formed themselves into a council and worked toward healing the division. Their work failed. The separation continued.

Cumberland Presbytery Reorganized

Finis Ewing, Samuel King, and Samuel McAdow, ordained ministers, were leaders of the council. Finis Ewing wanted to reorganize Cumberland Presbytery and seek membership again in Kentucky Synod. A meeting was held to make the decision. Finis Ewing, Samuel King, and Ephraim McLean (not yet ordained), visited Samuel McAdow on February 3, 1810. He lived near present-day Dickson, Tennessee. They asked McAdow to join with them in the reorganization. He refused to do so without first asking God's guidance. After a night in prayer, McAdow said he was ready. The three ministers formed Cumberland Presbytery and ordained Ephraim McLean. The day was February 4, 1810.

A New Church Is Born

They did not intend to begin a new denomination. They hoped still for reunion with Kentucky Synod. Their efforts failed. During the next three years, several new ministers and churches joined Cumberland Presbytery. In 1813, two other presbyteries and a synod were organized. Growth continued at such a rate that a General Assembly was organized in 1829. A new church had come into being!

Expansion and Growth

The next several years told an exciting story of growth. Schools were organized. New mission fields were opened, including work with Choctaw Indians in Mississippi. New congregations were begun in country and city. Great numbers of ministers were ordained. The church spread over many parts of the country. Within nineteen years after its founding the church had reached into eight states. By 1860, eight more states and a territory were added. By the end of the first century of its life, the denomination included twenty-five states.

The Denomination and the Civil War

As the church grew it also became more wise. During the Civil War, when other denominations were being split into North and South, the Cumberland Presbyterian denomination remained together. In view of the strong feelings of that period, this unit was a miracle.

A Separation

Following the Civil War, there was a separation which gave birth to another new denomination. Before the war, Cumberland Presbyterian congregations evangelized the slaves owned by their members. They were a part of the churches and attended worship. In addition, the Cumberland Presbyterian denomination ordained black preachers to preach to their own people separately from time to time. At the close of the war, there were perhaps twenty thousand black Cumberland Presbyterians.

After a few years, relationships between the white and black people changed. The General Assembly recognized the need for continued work with black Cumberland Presbyterians. At the same time the question of a separate church for black people arose. White and black Cumberland Presbyterians agreed that a separate church would be desirable. In 1869, the General Assembly heard a request from a convention of black Cumberland Presbyterians for a separate organization. This request was granted and a new Cumberland Presbyterian denomination came into being. The story of this church is told in Chapter V.

(Begin to work on the activities "To Learn More" and "Some Possible Activities" on page 34.)

CHAPTER IV
The Growth and Renewal of the Cumberland Presbyterian Denomination
(1883-Today)

The official seal of the General Assembly of the Cumberland Presbyterian Church was adopted by General Assembly in 1957. It features the Celtic Cross upon a trefoil within the encircling lettering, "General Assembly of the Cumberland Presbyterian Church—Founded 1810." The original Celtic Cross dates back to the 10th century, A. D., where it stood on the grounds of Iona Abbey in Scotland. With the passing of the years it has become the chief symbol of Presbyterianism.

A Picture History

The following pages show in pictures some of the work of our denomination following the Civil War. For a longer history of our church in the latter part of the 1800s and in the 1900s, see the books listed at the end of the chapter.

A New Confession of Faith

In 1810, Cumberland Presbytery used the Westminster Confession, written in 1649. It contains statements of belief widely accepted by Presbyterians for many generations. In 1814, the new church adopted a revision of the Westminster Confession. This revision reflected the influence of the Great Revival movement in the church.

In 1883, a new revision was written, saying more simply what the church believed. Both the Cumberland Presbyterian and Second Cumberland Presbyterian denominations have used this Confession. In 1984 the two denominations adopted the proposed revision of the Confession of Faith for our day.

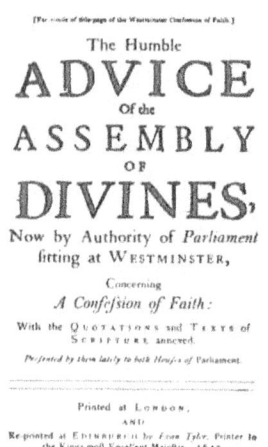
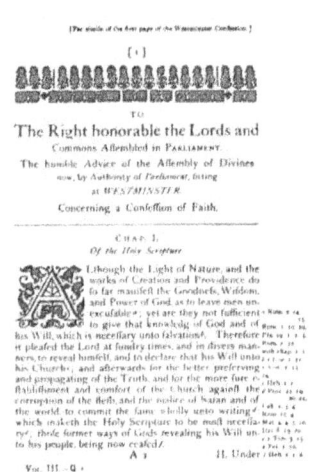

Westminster Confession of Faith

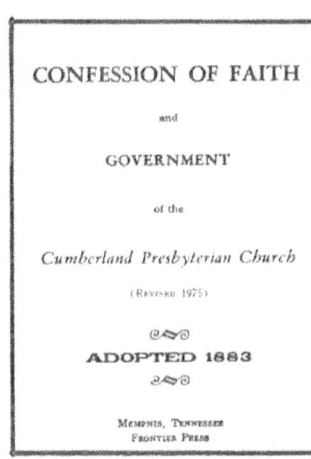

1883 Confession of Faith

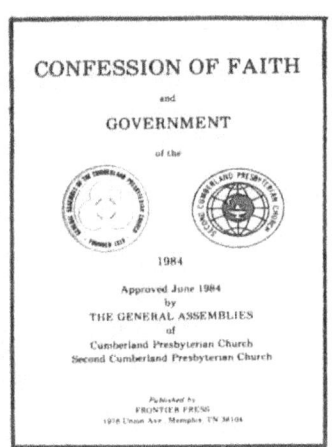

1984 Confession of Faith

Church Union

In the late 1800s many in the church came to feel that it had finished its mission as a separate denomination. At various times, union was discussed with the Presbyterian Church in the U.S., the Central Synod of the Evangelical Lutheran Church, the Presbyterian Church in the U.S.A., and the Methodist Protestant Church. A decision was made in 1906 to join the Presbyterian Church in the U.S.A. A large number of people did not want the union. They decided to continue the Cumberland Presbyterian denomination.

Rebuilding

Most of the Cumberland Presbyterian property went to the Presbyterian Church in the U.S.A. when the union was formed. Those who wished the Cumberland Presbyterian Church to continue had to rebuild it. It was much smaller in number and strength than it was before the union.

New Life—On the Frontier Again

In the 1930s and 1940s a new spirit began to work in the church. The denomination was reorganized in the late 1940s. New plans for growth and expansion were made. It marked a new beginning for the church.

After World War II many changes came in the world. Our church was made up of smaller congregations. None were very strong. It had congregations in nineteen states. How could it serve best in the changing world?

Our denomination from its beginning on the frontier was concerned with serving the world of which it was a part. It was willing to speak and work in new ways under God's leadership. When faced with a different world in the 1940s and 1950s, it did what our church founders did. It tried new things. The picture shows some of the new things it did.

Cumberland Presbyterian Center

The Center was built in 1950-51 with money given through the Program of Achievement, a plan designed by the Board of Finance to raise money for special needs. The Center became the headquarters for the entire church. A new building, named the Eugene Warren Building, was added in 1981. The Center is located at 1978 Union Avenue, Memphis, Tennessee.

Cumberland Presbyterian Center   **Eugene Warren Building**

Cumberland Presbyterian Children's Home

The Children's Home has been serving since 1912. It is located in Denton, Texas. It serves children in need of a home in which to live. As in other families, they are given love, care, recreation, Christian nurture, and education.

Children's Home Administration Building   **Mealtime at Children's Home**

Bethel College

Bethel College was founded in 1842 at McLemoresville, Tennessee. In 1872 it was moved to McKenzie, Tennessee. It gives young people a good liberal arts education. Some courses help them prepare to enter a profession—like medicine or law, the ministry or teaching. The campus is attractive and the people are friendly. Every student receives special attention.

Bethel College Administration Building

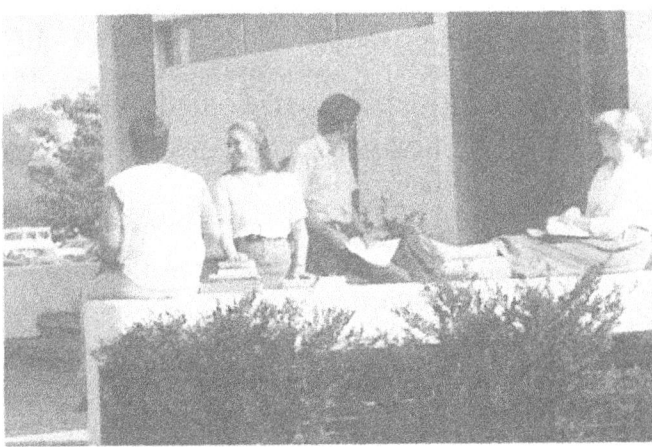
Bethel Students at Burroughs Learning Center

Christian Education

The work of Christian Education was begun in the 1920s by the Board of Publication. In 1927 a Board of Young People's Work was organized. The Reverend Clark Williamson began serving as General Secretary. This Board was replaced in 1936 by a Board of Christian Education. The work was enlarged.

Christian Education includes Sunday school, children, youth, adults, family life, camps and conferences.

Classroom Drama

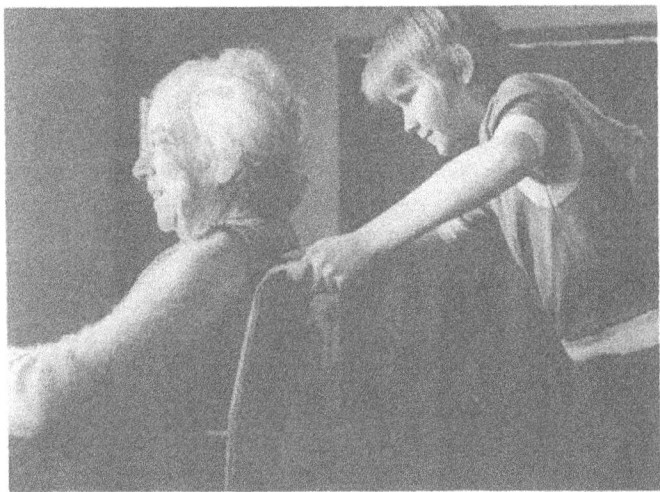
A Child Helping Others

Classroom Art Activity Studying the Wonders of Nature

New Church Development

As people move and their numbers increase in certain regions of the nation, new churches have to be built. The Board of Missions is in charge of this work. Today new churches are being organized in many parts of our denomination.

An Addition to a Church

The Church at Work in China, South America, Hong Kong, and Japan

After 1906, the church began new mission work for people in countries other than ours. Mission work began in Canton, China, in 1918. A mission field was opened in Colombia, South America, in 1925. The work around Canton was destroyed by the Communists after World War II. New work was started in Hong Kong. In 1949 a mission was organized in Tokyo, Japan.

The Gam Sing Quah Family

Organization of Hong Kong Presbytery

Jose and Fanny Fajardo

Hot Lunch Program in Colombia

Koza Church, Tokyo, Japan

30th Anniversary Celebration in Japan

Memphis Theological Seminary

Throughout its history, the Cumberland Presbyterian Church has been interested in the education of ministers—theological education. Before 1906, several theological schools were started. After the reunion, efforts were begun almost at once to organize a theological school in connection with Bethel College. A seminary program was maintained on the Bethel campus until 1964, when it was moved to Memphis. In its new home, the seminary has grown in terms of faculty, students, library, and outreach.

Memphis Theological Seminary

MTS Students and Faculty

Giving Our Money

The Lord's work calls for careful use of money and unselfish giving. The Board of Finance guides the church in handling its money. It helps raise money for Our United Outreach. This money pays for the work of the various agencies of the church. It teaches people Christian giving. It encourages people to leave money to the church through their wills. It lends money to new churches. It helps congregations to plan for better giving.

To Learn More

To learn more about the denomination use the following questions as a guide. Your pastor will be able to help you.

How many ordained ministers do we have?

How many congregations are in our denomination?

How many members are listed in our records?

In what states do we have congregations?

What is a presbytery? How many do we have?

What is a synod? How many synods do we have?

What is the General Assembly? (Both Cumberland Presbyterian denominations have a General Assembly.)

In what presbytery and synod is your congregation located?

What are our church's institutions?

What are the names of the denominational boards? What is their work?

Record this information in your "Log for Journey of Faith."

Some Possible Activities

Make a time line of Cumberland Presbyterian history. Start it with the Revival of 1800. List dates and events through the present day.

Make murals of historical events in the history of the Cumberland Presbyterian Church. You might include the reorganization of Cumberland Presbytery or a camp meeting.

Make a church Hall of Fame. Sketch people from our history. Write briefly about what they did, where it was done, and when.

With the help of your pastor, draw a chart showing the relation of your congregation to presbytery, synod, and general assembly.

Jargon for the Journey

DENOMINATION: An organization of Christian people and congregations who have the same beliefs, purposes, practices, and government. Examples: the Cumberland Presbyterian Church and Second Cumberland Presbyterian Church.

ORDINATION: The act of setting apart a man or woman for special service in the church. Lay people are ordained as ruling elders by the congregation. They serve on the church session. Ministers are ordained as teaching elders by the presbytery. The person being ordained kneels and the other elders or ministers place their hands on his or her head. Someone leads in prayer. Ordination gives a person certain rights and responsibilities. These privileges and duties are similar for ruling elders and teaching elders, though they are not all the same.

INSTITUTION: An organization which helps fill special needs of people. It may be a school, a church, a hospital, a nursing home, a children's home.

PRESBYTERY: A presbytery is made up of a group of congregations and ministers in a special area. Each congregation elects at least one elder to represent (speak and act for) it when presbytery meets. Presbytery guides the work of its congregations and ministers. Most presbyteries meet twice a year.

SYNOD: Three or more presbyteries are grouped together as a synod. A synod includes the presbyteries within a certain state, part of a state, or some larger area. Its purpose is to guide the work of the presbyteries and to encourage support of the work of the whole denomination.

GENERAL ASSEMBLY: A church body made up of commissioners (ministers and ruling elders) elected by presbyteries to speak and act for them. The General Assembly guides the work of the entire denomination. It meets once every year.

CHURCH BOARD: A church board is a group of persons elected by presbytery, synod or General Assembly to carry on special work such as Christian education, missions, money management, or operation of church institutions.

EVANGELISM: Spreading the gospel through every means to as many people as possible. Some means of evangelism are person to person, teaching, preaching, revivals, television, radio, and printed materials.

CONFESSION OF FAITH: Statements of belief made by a church denomination. A confession is usually printed in a book, like the Confession of Faith of the Cumberland Presbyterian Church.

OUR UNITED OUTREACH: The program of raising and budgeting money for the work of the Cumberland Presbyterian Church. Each presbytery accepts a suggested amount of money to be raised each year. Congregations are asked to give to reach this goal.

Resources

The materials listed here will give you more information about our church. They will help you answer some of your questions.

Good News on the Frontier, Thomas H. Campbell, Frontier Press, 1965
A People Called Cumberland Presbyterians, Baugh, Barrus, Campbell, Frontier Press, 1972
General Assembly Minutes (published every year)
Yearbook of the General Assembly (published every year)

CHAPTER V
The History and Mission of the Second Cumberland Presbyterian Denomination

The seal for the Second Cumberland Presbyterian Church symbolizes "The Church Commissioned to Bear Witness to the Light of the World to All Who Will Receive."

Black People in America

The school day is just beginning. Students stand, place their right hand over their hearts, and recite the pledge to the flag.

"I pledge allegiance to the flag of the United States of America, and to the republic for which it stands; one nation, under God, indivisible, with liberty and justice for all."

Public school children repeat the pledge to the American flag on a regular basis. Students learn to respect the flag. They know it is a symbol, standing for something that is very important.

Here is another kind of flag. It, too, stands for something. It, too, is very important to Americans, especially black Americans.

The flag is called an "Afro-American flag." It has three colors, and each color holds a very special meaning.

The red in the flag symbolizes past, present, and future suffering for dignity and freedom. The black symbolizes black people. The green symbolizes hope for justice and freedom. The story of black Americans is one of suffering and hope.

Black Cumberland Presbyterians have a story of suffering and hope. This chapter tells a part of that story. The story begins during the time of slavery.

The Church Begins

Before the Civil War (1861-1865), many members of the Cumberland Presbyterian Church owned slaves. These slaves often worshiped in the same churches as the owners. Many chose to join the Cumberland Presbyterian Church.

Sometimes the slaves worshiped God in their own groups. Let's take an imaginary trip back in time to 1860. That's over 120 years ago.

As we walk through the countryside, we begin to hear singing in the distance. As we get closer, we hear the music getting louder and louder. Soon, we see a group of people singing. Let us listen closely to the words of their songs.

Chorus: Bye and bye, I'm gonna lay
   down dis heavy load.
   O I been 'buked and I been scorned.
   Done had a hard time sho's you born.

Chorus: Oh, nobody knows de trouble I've
   seen,
   Nobody knows but Jesus.
   Nobody knows de trouble I've seen,
   Glory hallelujah.
   Sometimes I'm up, sometimes I'm
      down,
   Oh, yes, Lord;
   Sometimes I'm almost to de groun',
   Oh, yes, Lord.

After that song has been sung, another person rises and begins to sing:

Steal a-way, steal a-way;
Steal a-way to Jesus;
Steal a-way, steal a-way,
I ain't got long to stay here.

These songs, called spirituals, talk about suffering, trouble, sorrow, and hope. The songs point out a desire to be released from slavery. The songs also reflect a strong faith in God. Because of this strong religious faith, the slaves learned to live with hope despite the conditions.

Five years later, it is 1865. The United States has just ended an ugly war called the Civil War. One reason there was a war was that United States citizens disagreed about whether persons could own slaves. The Civil War was won by those who were against slavery. So, all slaves, including those who were Cumberland Presbyterians, were freed after the war.

Now, in 1865, the country is trying to bind up its wounds, rebuild, and re-unite. The Emancipation Proclamation, which became effective January 1, 1863, freed the slaves, and the Thirteenth Amendment to the Constitution of the United States of America, put an end to all forms of slavery in the country.

The slave-owner relationship ended. No longer did black people have to get permission from white people for anything. Black people could now make their own decisions. They alone determined what they would do with their lives.

The experience of independence was new to the slaves. For most of them, freedom had only been an idea and a dream. Perhaps few understood the full meaning of freedom, but suddenly, they were free! "What shall we do with our freedom?" was their cry.

Should black Cumberland Presbyterians continue to worship with their former owners, or should they begin a denomination of their own? The decision was not an easy one to make. It took nine years. Starting in 1865, black church leaders discussed this question. It was 1874 when they reached their decision.

But, let's go to 1868. We find ourselves in Henderson, Kentucky. A convention is held to decide what should be done. Let us listen in on that meeting.

FIRST MINISTER (*standing*): Let us bow our heads in prayer. Dear God, we come before thee and in thy holy presence to ask thy guidance as we consider our future. Lead us as we make our choice. Help us to listen for thy direction. In the Name of thy Son, we pray. Amen.

ALL: Amen.

FIRST MINISTER: Brethren, we have met here to make some important decisions about our future. The question before us is, "Shall we continue to worship with our former slave owners, or shall we start on a journey which will lead to the birth of a separate denomination?" I invite each of you to speak to this question.

SECOND MINISTER: Mr. Chairman, for some time now, we have not worshiped with our white brethren. While we need to continue to love our former owners and all others of a different race, I believe the time has come for us to establish ourselves as a separate church. Let's try to hold as many of the twenty thousand members as we can. (As he sits, several in attendance nod their heads in agreement.)

THIRD MINISTER: Mr. Chairman, we need to think about this very important point: Just how long do you think we will last if we separate ourselves from our white brothers? We have no church building, few books and Bibles, a handful of ordained ministers who know about the government of the church. We have not been taught enough yet to go out on our own. If we go out alone now, in a few years, we will be out of existence and completely forgotten. I, for one, believe we need to stay a while longer. (As he sits, several in attendance nod their heads in agreement.)

FOURTH MINISTER: True, we have very little in material things, but if we have the will, we can make it with the help of God.

No definite decision was reached in that meeting. This meeting ended with an agreement to return a year later and with a commitment to make a firm choice about the future.

In January, 1869, in Huntsville, Alabama, another meeting was held. Again, no decision was reached. A third meeting was scheduled.

In May, 1869, in Murfreesboro, Tennessee, during the time the General Assembly of the

Cumberland Presbyterian Church was meeting, a full delegation of black Cumberland Presbyterians met separately to consider their future. In this meeting, a decision was reached. It was communicated to the General Assembly by the Rev. Moses Weir.

REV. MR. WEIR: Our fathers and our brothers, I come before you today not to represent myself, but to represent the more than 20,000 black freed slaves who proudly call themselves Cumberland Presbyterians. We thank God for the great tradition you have given us. We love the Cumberland Presbyterian Church. It is a strong doctrine. We think there is none better in all the earth. It has a strong government. As persons who believe in making our own decisions, we like a church government which calls for a democracy. We thank you for what you have given us. Blessed be the Lord for all his benefits.

As you know, we have convened a meeting of many of our ministers and elders alongside the meeting of this General Assembly. Just one hour ago, we reached a major decision which I have been asked to communicate to you. My fellow ministers have asked me to be the spokesman for this occasion.

Your black brothers, who also proudly call themselves Cumberland Presbyterians, have decided to organize a Colored Cumberland Presbyterian Church. We feel that it would not be for the achievement of the church, among either of the races, for our ministers to continue to be in the same church at this time.

In order for us to be organized as a denomination, we request the following of you: (1) that you organize black Cumberland Presbyterians into separate presbyteries and synods; (2) that you make available to us some church buildings so that we might have places for worship; (3) that you make available to us some hymn books and Bibles; and (4) that you help us secure a school for the education of our ministers.

Since our relationship has been cordial, we ask that you assist us as we start on this journey of faith. If you help us in these four ways, we believe that our church can make it.

All the leaders of the church send their greetings and wish for you a most blessed meeting of the General Assembly. May God bless you all.

The General Assembly of the Cumberland Presbyterian Church acted favorably to fill the requests.

Elk River Presbytery was the first presbytery in the new church. Organized in 1869, it included the congregations that were in Middle Tennessee. In 1871, Hopewell Presbytery of West Tennessee and Greenville Presbytery were organized. These three presbyteries made up the first synod, called the Tennessee Synod. By the end of 1873, seven presbyteries had been organized.

The most eventful day was yet to come. It finally arrived on May 1, 1874. The place was Nashville, Tennessee. The occasion was the first meeting of the General Assembly of the Colored Cumberland Presbyterian Church.* Let us listen in on this meeting, presided over by the Rev. Pink Price, the first moderator of the General Assembly of the new denomination.

THE MODERATOR: Mr. Stated Clerk, the Rev. J. F. Humphrey; commissioners; friends: the first General Assembly of the Colored Cumberland Presbyterian Church is now in session *(sounding of gavel twice)*. Let us pray.

Be with us, O Lord God, as we convene the first General Assembly of the Colored Cumberland Presbyterian Church. Guide us as we begin this journey. We realize that the road ahead may be rocky, but with thy help, we will make it. We ask this in the name of thy Son and our Savior, Jesus Christ. Amen.

ALL (standing): Amen. Amen. Amen. (They all stand and sing without music, "I Love Thy Church, O God.")

THE STATED CLERK: The roll call of presbyteries: Please stand as I call the name of your presbytery. Huntsville. (*The commissioners from Huntsville Presbytery stand.*) Elk River. (*Commissioners stand.*) Farmington. Hiwassee. New Hopewell. New Middleton. Springfield.

FIRST COMMISSIONER TO SPEAK: Mr. Moderator and brethren of this great assembly, I am happy to report on behalf of the committee on statistics the following information. We have 46 ordained min-

---

*The name Colored Cumberland Presbyterian Church was used for many years. In 1960 the name was changed to the Second Cumberland Presbyterian Church.

isters; 20 ministers licensed to preach; 30 candidates for the ministry; 3,000 members.

The new church was born. Its beginnings were modest. It had but a small membership.

By 1886, twelve years after that first General Assembly, the statistics of the young church included 200 ordained ministers, 225 licensed to preach, 200 candidates, 25 presbyteries, four synods, and 13,000 members.

Young and struggling it was, but the church had begun!

The Young Church Grows Up

As the years passed, the young church became more and more aware of its independence. The time was fast approaching for it to stop thinking backward to the beginnings. Indeed, time had come for it to plan its future and strengthen itself for growth.

The church is people. The church is not a building nor a series of buildings. Rather, the church is people. The story of this new, growing church is the story of struggles and hopes of people.

Local Churches Serve People

Though slavery no longer existed and black Cumberland Presbyterians had their own churches, the story of suffering and hope continued.

Freedom from slavery was good. The freed slaves thanked God for that. But, life for them was still very hard.

> Into the world he (freedman) went alone,
> Stumbling and struggling in paths unknown;
> Is it strange that his future seemed dark and dim,
> And dark to us as it was to him?

Think about the situation of the freed slaves. They owned no property. They had no education. They had no homes. The sky was the roof over their heads. The ground was their bed.

Local churches played a very important role for the freed persons. Some would have given up, but the church helped them keep hope alive, reminding them that "soon and very soon, life was going to be better."

Religious worship was very important to them. Some had experienced hard times as slaves. In many cases, parents were separated from their children; husbands were separated from wives. The memories could not be recalled without sadness. It was not unusual for the worship services to be filled with outbursts of feelings, such as crying aloud, screaming, and walking back and forth during the service.

Local churches gave comfort and security to the people. There people care for each other. Close friendships were developed. Many who were afraid of the present and the future could share their hurts, worries, and fears with other persons who cared.

The following song was often sung in their worship services:

> While my spirit was wandering around,
>   My God sent a little angel down;
> Plucked my feet from the miry clay,
>   Set them on the rock of eternal age;
> God sent a written letter unto me,
>   The reading on the letter said: "You are free."
> In the school of grace you'll read and learn,
>   You are plucked as brand from eternal burn.
> Chorus: I've got religion, yes, yes;
>   and the world can do me no harm.

As the chorus was repeated several times in a long mourn, the congregation would join in the singing, keeping time with their hands, heads, feet, and bodies.

Religious faith and life in the community of faith were major reasons many of the freed slaves were able to live life successfully.

Ministers Give Good Leadership

Key persons in this new church were the ministers. They were helpful in guiding the former slaves through troublesome times.

Among the first ministers ordained by the white church to preach in the black denomination were Lewis Neal, Samuel Fumbanks, Hamp Jones, and Pink Price. These men and others organized new churches wherever they could, and the church spread to many parts of the south.

As examples of the ministers in this church, we will examine the lives of four—James B. Sadler, Elijah Simpson, J. M. D. DeShong, and C. L. Davis.

Rev. James B. Sadler

Rev. Elijah Simpson

Rev. J. M. W. DeShong

Rev. C. L. Davis

James B. Sadler: The church had its beginning west of the Mississippi in 1870. Several congregations were organized in Texas. Shortly afterward, Rev. J. Y. Estelle of Harrison, Texas, Rev. I. Snowden from Bush Chapel at Elm Mott, and Rev. James B. Sadler of Bosque County requested permission of Waco Presbytery of the Cumberland Presbyterian church to begin a separate presbytery. Brazos River Presbytery was duly organized and met for the first time on February 4, 1877.

James B. Sadler (1828-1911) was the son of a slave owner and a slave woman. He was brought to Bosque County, Texas, from Tennessee by a medical doctor named Sadler, who is assumed to have been his father. James Sadler founded and built the first Colored Cumberland Presbyterian Church in Texas, the Rock Springs Church. That church still stands today.

Elijah Simpson: A leader in the Kentucky area of the church was Rev. Dr. Elijah Simpson. Dr. Simpson was born in Crittenden County, Kentucky, October 2, 1852. The first plans for his education were laid by the young children of his master and a Mrs. M. A. Williams.

He began his study as a student for the ministry in 1869. In 1871, he was ordained by Green River Presbytery. Only nineteen years old at the time, he began a life of preaching and teaching. In 1870, he taught his first school; in 1874, he taught the first public school in Hopkins County, Kentucky, for the instruction of black children. In 1902, Cadiz Normal and Theological College of Cadiz, Kentucky, conferred on him an honorary doctor of divinity degree.

He served as moderator of the General Assembly when he was thirty years old.

J. M. W. DeShong: Rev. J. M. W. DeShong was born in North Carolina, January 9, 1853. He and his parents were brought to Tennessee by their owners in 1859. In August 1870, he professed faith in Jesus Christ, and joined the Colored Cumberland Presbyterian Church. He joined the Hopewell Presbytery on September 18, 1871, and was licensed to preach the gospel on March 25, 1872, at Huntingdon, Tennessee.

DeShong moved to Milan, Tennessee, in 1873 where he resided with his mother and sister. He organized ten churches. He served as clerk of Walton Presbytery, West Tennessee Synod. He edited and published *The Colored Cumberland Presbyterian,* the church paper. Faithful and earnest, as he grew in age, he grew in wisdom, and the work of the denomination was largely guided by his work during his adult life.

C. L. Davis: Rev. C. L. Davis was born in

Alabama. He was reared on a farm and was acquainted with manual labor. He professed Christian religion at the age of fifteen, joined the church and made it known that he wanted to become a minister.

Davis took private lessons in theology under a very able instructor who declared that he was an apt student. His formal education began late in life; about the age of eighteen, he boarded the train for the first time en route to Huntsville, Alabama, where he entered the State Normal School.

As an ordained minister, he built several churches, the most prominent of which is the Pratt City Church, Birmingham, which he pastored for twelve years.

Schools

Efforts to provide for training of ministers began early in the life of this young church. Several training institutions were founded, including schools at Bowling Green, Kentucky; Springfield, Missouri; Huntsville, Alabama; and Newbern, Tennessee. Each of these schools failed because of the lack of financial support.

To maintain schools and a publishing house required money, more money than the young church could raise. The denomination was made up of people who earned little money. They worked hard, but they did not earn much take-home pay. They had little to give to the church.

Prior to the 1950's, working black men earned very little money in the South where most of the church members lived. Low levels of income slowed the work of the black church. Many of the young church's dreams ended in nightmares because there was no money to accomplish them.

Headquarters

As early as the turn of the twentieth century, the church wanted to build a place where it could publish its materials and carry on its denominational work. A central location for all denominational doings was needed.

In the 1950's, Alabama Synod began publishing a monthly bulletin and rented an office in the city of Huntsville for its clerk and publisher, Rev. E. D. White. A few years later, Second Cumberland Presbyterian Church, Huntsville, built an addition to its church building and provided space for White to work. He also served as the pastor of that church.

In 1959, the synod invited the General Assembly to join the project and utilize the facilities of the synod and to allow it to become national headquarters. The offer was

Dedication of New Headquarters Building

The Cumberland Flag

accepted, and the General Assembly began to give money for that use.

Since larger facilities were needed, the General Assembly kept looking for a better place and method for doing its work. Finally, in 1976, the church built a headquarters building in Huntsville, and by October, 1976, the building was in use.

The Church in the Eighties

When the 1980s began, the denomination consisted of 6,494 members divided among 143 congregations in fifteen presbyteries and four synods. The General Assembly is organized with three boards: Board of Missions and Evangelism, Board of Christian Education and Publication, and Board of Finance. The women's work, called the Second Cumberland Presbyterian Women, contributes many services to the denomination. There is an organized youth program at the General Assembly level, called National Youth Work. The National Sunday School Convention directs the work of Sunday schools in the church. A monthly publication, *The Cumberland Flag,* is the communication arm of the church.

The largest area numerically is Alabama Synod. It has five presbyteries which make up nearly one-third of the entire church. East and Middle Tennessee areas have large numbers of Cumberland Presbyterians. The church extends as far north as Detroit, Cleveland, and Chicago; as far west as Marshalltown, Iowa, and Dallas; as far south as Selma, Alabama. The church is located primarily in the southeastern United States.

Joint Committee on Unification Logo

The General Assembly meets once each year. The moderator is elected in each meeting. The stated clerk is elected every three years.

The story of suffering and of hope has continued into the 1980s. The daily experience of black people continues to include suffering. The church, especially at the local level, continues to be compassionate and help its mem-

Joint Committee on Unification in Session

National Youth Work Session

bers to live in hope. In many cases, Sunday worship services and periods of fellowship scheduled at other times provide opportunities for sufferings to be shared and hope to be renewed. In worship, people sing, play, affirm one another, and share each other's struggles, troubles, and social concerns.

At present, the two Cumberland Presbyterian denominations have a Joint Committee on Unification and look toward possible reunion as soon as 1993. A number of cooperative activities have developed between the two denominations since 1950—notably in Christian education, youth ministry, college and seminary instruction, and the proposed revision of the *Confession of Faith*. Other ways of working together are continually being explored at all levels of the denominations.

Whether or not reunion occurs, the relationship between black and white Cumberland Presbyterians serves to remind us all of the unity and diversity in the body of Christ, the church universal.

CHAPTER VI
Our Relation To Other Denominations

The boat is a symbol for Christ's whole church. We are in it together.
People from all parts of the earth are one in Christ.

Our Relation To Other Denominations
"All one body we"

A Fantasy About E. T.

In 1982 E. T. came to earth. At first he scared us. But we all came to love him. He taught us to trust each other.

But his visit was so short! And limited to only a few people. He had too little time to see what the earth was really like or learn much about us.

He was treated so kindly by the family he visited he wanted to come back to the earth again. After long months of asking, his people finally consented for him to return briefly.

The family he visited were Cumberland Presbyterians. Among the topics of conversation was the church. E. T. did not know anything about the church or the story of Jesus. The words and symbols he used to describe his religion were different.

They took him to see the church they attended. On the way there and back he saw many church buildings. He began to ask questions. The more he asked, the more they tried to explain, the more confused E. T. became.

If everyone worshiped the same God, and believed in Jesus, how come there were so many churches?

Suppose E. T. came to visit your town and family. How would you explain why there are so many denominations?

This chapter may help you with E. T.—and other seekers.

The Church Is One, Yet Divided

The church of Jesus Christ is one. Yet it is broken into many parts. It has people of various ages, races, nations, and cultures. It reaches around the world. It is many. Yet it is one. In this chapter we will look at some of these parts of the church and ask how we can relate to them.

"Onward, Christian Soldiers" sings of the unity of Christ's church:
*"We are not divided, All one body we,
One in hope and doctrine, One in charity."*

"Blest Be the Tie" sings of other ways in which we are one:
*"Before our Father's throne
We pour our ardent prayers;
Our fears, our hopes, our aims are one,
Our comforts and our cares."*

We are one. And yet we are divided.

The early Christians had disagreements. Paul wrote about the division in the congregation in Corinth. "Is Christ divided?" he asked. Four parties had been formed. Some members followed Paul as the true leader. Others followed Apollos. Still others followed Peter. Some wanted to follow only Christ. Read 1 Corinthians 1:10-13; 3:1-9. Paul stated that Christ is one and the church is one. We all should learn to work together.

The letter to the Ephesians develops the same theme. In 2:11-22, the writer reports how Christ broke down the walls of separation. He brought Jews and Gentiles together. In 4:1-6, the writer says all Christians are united. "There is one body and one Spirit . . . one hope . . . one Lord, one faith, one baptism, one God and Father of us all. . . ."

A long prayer of Jesus is recorded in John 17. In verses 20-23, he prays for unity so people will believe. ". . . that they will all be one; even as thou, Father, art in me, and I in thee, that they also may be in us, so that the world may believe that thou hast sent me" (verse 21).

How the Church Became Divided

Examine the tree of the Christian church below. It shows some of the major branches and when they were formed. Take time to get the picture clearly in your mind.

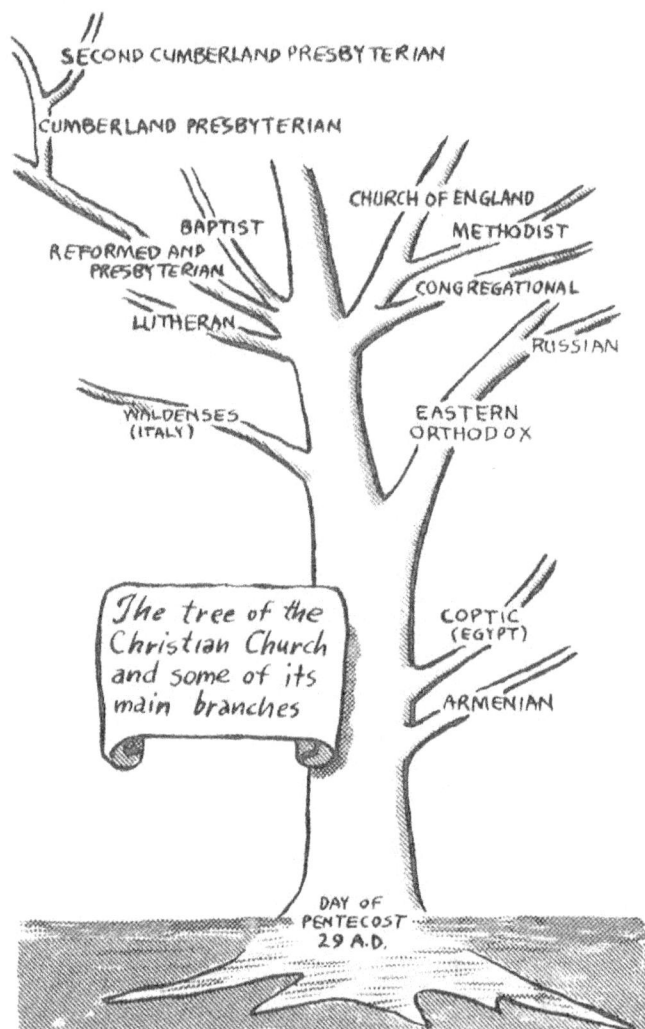

The first separation from the main tree was made by the Armenian Christians. We are told this church was founded by the apostles Thaddaeus and Bartholomew. Armenia became the first Christian state. In the latter part of the fifth century, Armenian Christians became a separate branch of the church. It happened over a dispute about the nature of Jesus Christ. They rejected the teaching that Jesus was both human and divine. They believed that he was only divine.

The Coptic Church of Egypt split from the main body about the same time over beliefs and politics. They, too, believed only in the divine nature of Christ. Both the Armenians and Copts continue today as active churches.

As time passed the church became stronger. Christians of the Eastern and Western areas began to compete with each other for influence. In 1054 the church was divided into two sections. Constantinople (now Istanbul) became the headquarters for Christians in the east. This branch became the Eastern Orthodox Church. From it came later the Greek and Russian Orthodox churches.

Rome became the headquarters for the Christians in the west. Rome continues as the central place of control for Roman Catholics. The Bishop of Rome finally came to be regarded as the Pope. He is the head of this branch of the church. The Roman Church became very wealthy. It also came to have great influence in the world.

In the latter part of the twelfth century, Peter Waldo started a reform movement. He preached that people should live in simple ways. He was put out of the Roman Church by the Council of Verona. His followers organized and continued as a separate branch. They are called the Waldenses. They tried hard to live by the spirit and teachings of Jesus Christ. Their church spread rapidly into southern France, northern Italy, Spain, and central Europe. They were mistreated for centuries because of their religion. They still exist as a separate group.

Some leaders in the Roman Church did not lead the church spiritually. Many Christians tried to bring the church back to the beliefs and practices of the early followers of Jesus. They were unable to do so. The Roman Church grew in influence and wealth. The church was ruled by bishops and archbishops. The people had little to say in ruling their own lives.

In the early part of the sixteenth century Martin Luther of Germany stirred the people to oppose the wrongs in the church. A movement began called the Reformation. Out of it came many other branches of the church. Some of them were Lutherans and the Presbyterian and Reformed Churches. Others came later.

Following the Reformation, leaders in the Roman Church began a movement to improve conditions. Many things were changed for the better. In recent years a Council held in Rome by Pope John XXIII brought better understanding between the Roman Catholic and Protestant churches.

As the result of the separations through the years there are more than three hundred branches of the church. Some refuse to accept others. Some groups will work with a few other groups. Many carry on their work alone. Large numbers of churches work together in many ways. They share their knowledge in mission work. They prepare study courses and materials for Christian education. They work for justice and peace. They seek ways of helping the poor.

Some of these branches of the church may be in your community. You will want to learn more about them. How many of the churches listed below are in your community? Put a check mark by those which are.

_____ An Episcopal Church
_____ A Lutheran Church (Lutherans have more than one denomination, like American Lutherans, Missouri Synod Lutherans, The Lutheran Church in America.)
_____ A Presbyterian Church (other than Cumberland)
_____ A Reformed Church
_____ A United Church of Christ (not Church of Christ)
_____ A Methodist Church (There are several Methodist denominations, like United Methodist, African Methodist Episcopal, Christian Methodist Episcopal.)

_____ A Baptist Church (There are many Baptist denominations, like Southern Baptists, American Baptists, Primitive Baptists.)
_____ The Church of Christ
_____ A Christian Church (Disciples of Christ)
_____ A Nazarene Church
_____ A Church of God (made up of more than one denomination)
_____ An Assembly of God (made up of more than one denomination)
_____ A Mormon Church (the Church of Jesus Christ of Latter Day Saints)
_____ Others (like Brethren, Mennonite, Moravian, Friends)

How much do you know about the churches which are in your community? When did their denominations begin? When was the congregation organized? What are their beliefs? What kind of worship do they have? What kind of work do they do in serving the community? In what ways are they different from the Cumberland Presbyterian Church? In what ways are they like the Cumberland Presbyterian Church? Do they work with other churches? Does your congregation work with any of them? In what ways?

If you want to learn more about any of these churches, ask your pastor or class leader to help you. You may have in your school, church, or public library a book which will give you more information.

There may be religious groups in your community which are not Christian. Jews are one such group in many North American communities. Do you know of any other non-Christian religious group in your town or country?

Relating to Other Churches

Now we come to ask what our attitudes toward other churches are to be. It is easy to work with and accept those whose beliefs are like our own. It is more difficult when they are different. We may find it easy to think another church is wrong if it does not believe as we believe. We may even reject the people in churches that do not agree with us. We may forget that they are human beings of worth whom God created and loves.

One of the questions often asked by young Christians is: Who is right and who is wrong in their beliefs? Are we expected to choose one group as being right and to think all others are wrong? There are those who do this.

Remember that none of us is perfect. All of us are limited. At best we are sinners saved by God's grace. So there is no one group of people who can rightfully and sanely say their beliefs are absolutely right and true. We are all a mixture of strengths and weaknesses in faith and practice. There are truth and error in all churches. At best we represent a part of the whole truth.

The Cumberland Presbyterian denominations have usually accepted and respected other churches. We have worked with some and not with others. We have given all people the right to their own beliefs. We have claimed that right for ourselves.

Here are some guidelines for relating to other churches and their people:

Learn all you can about other churches and their beliefs. Find out what they believe. Learn what they do in practicing their faith. Don't pass unfair and uninformed judgment on them. Don't accept what some people tell you about them. Read and study for yourself. Or ask people who are fair and well informed.

Respect other people and their religion. They have the right to believe as they do. Our country guarantees religious freedom. Don't mess it up. On the one hand, defend the right of all people to follow their conscience in faith and practice. Don't laugh at the way others worship. Don't make fun of their doctrine. Don't tell jokes about them or put them down in any way. Believe they are sincere. If you feel your faith is better and you would like to share it, do it humbly. On the other hand, demand that others respect your right to believe as you do. Question any unfair, untrue claim they may make about your faith. This can be done frankly and openly without hate or anger.

Work with other churches and groups whenever you can. You do not have to agree with everything others believe. You can join them to serve needs in the community and world in spite of this. Remember that the true faith is not in what you believe. It is loving and serving God and neighbor. These lines in "Faith of Our Fathers!" express the right attitude:

"Faith of our fathers! we will love
Both friend and foe in all our strife:
And preach thee, too, as love knows how,
By kindly words and virtuous life."

Conclusion

After reading this chapter and thinking about your relation to Christians in other denominations, give yourself a test on attitudes. Mark the following statements on a scale from 1 to 5. (1 is highest agreement. 5 is lowest agreement.)

All who believe in Jesus Christ are one people regardless of their denomination.	1 2 3 4 5
All who believe in Jesus Christ are brothers and sisters in him.	1 2 3 4 5
All Christians ought to relate to each other and work together as one family.	1 2 3 4 5
All Christians are due our love, understanding, and respect.	1 2 3 4 5

Having read this chapter, are you ready to write a brief statement of faith about relating to people of other denominations? Try it and see how it comes out. Record it in "Log for Journey of Faith."

Jargon for the Journey

GENTILES: Non-Jewish people. In the Bible, those who are not Jews are referred to as Gentiles.

ARMENIA: Now a small area in Russia, located between Russia, Iran, and Turkey.

COPTIC: Of the Copts, natives of Egypt descended from the ancient inhabitants of that country. Used to refer to the church made up of these people.

ORTHODOX: Proper or correct beliefs. Agreeing with the faith of Christians formed in the early creeds and confessions.

PROTESTANT: Those Christians who are not members of the Roman Catholic or Eastern Orthodox Church. The term applied also to those Christians separating from the Roman Catholic Church at the time of the Reformation.

BISHOP: In the early Christian era a person who was a spiritual overseer of the church. Now, and for a long time, a minister who is in charge of a church district or area.

A Helpful Book

Handbook of Denominations in the United States, Frank Mead, Abingdon Press, the Seventh Edition, 1980.

CHAPTER VII

The Bible

The symbol for the Bible is the open book. It stands for the Bible as the inspired Word of God, the true guide for Christian faith and practice.

A BIBLE QUIZ

Mark the following quotes. Mark **X** for those you think are from the Bible. Mark **O** for those you think are from some other source. Your teacher will give you the answers.

1. __ Let every vat stand upon its own bottom.
2. __ He found him in the waste howling wilderness.
3. __ Early to bed and early to rise, makes a man healthy, wealthy, and wise.
4. __ An old man is twice a child.
5. __ Finders keepers, losers weepers.
6. __ You brood of vipers! Who warned you to flee?
7. __ Man shall not live by bread alone.
8. __ A penny saved is a penny earned.
9. __ Judge not, and you will not be judged.
10. __ Bring the fatted calf and kill it.
11. __ Blessed are you that weep now, for you shall laugh.
12. __ Neither a borrower nor a lender be.
13. __ All that goes up is bound to come down.
14. __ Every cloud has its silver lining.
15. __ You shall know the truth, and the truth shall set you free.
16. __ You are the salt of the earth.
17. __ I came, I saw, I conquered.
18. __ A good name is to be chosen rather than great riches.
19. __ God helps them who help themselves.
20. __ Give instructions to a wise man, and he will be still wiser.

The Bible
The True Guide for Christian Faith and Practice

> Before reading this chapter, give yourself a test. Do you know the answers to the following questions?
> - What does the word Bible mean?
> - How many books are in the Old Testament? How many books in the New Testament?
> - How many books can you name? How many can you spell?
> - What does the word "testament" mean?
> - Who wrote the Bible?
> - How long did it take to write it?
> - What led the people to write the Bible?
> - The Bible is referred to as God's Word, the Word of God, the Scriptures. What do these terms mean?

Introduction

The Bible is the world's greatest book. A knowledge of the Bible is the mark of a truly educated person. Learning how to read and study it is necessary for an understanding of the Christian faith.

Read the following hymn. Underline the words referring to the Bible. What do these words say about the Bible and what it is like?

Thy Word is like a garden, Lord,
With flowers bright and fair;
And everyone who seeks may pluck
A lovely cluster there.
Thy Word is like a deep, deep mine;
And jewels rich and rare
Are hidden in its mighty depths
For every searcher there.

Thy Word is like a starry host;
A thousand rays of light
Are seen to guide the traveler,
And make his pathway bright.
Thy Word is like an armory,
Where soldiers may repair,
And find, for life's long battle day,
All needful weapons there.

Oh may I love Thy precious Word,
May I explore the mine,
May I its fragrant flowers glean,
May light upon me shine.
O may I find my armor there,
Thy Word my trusty sword;
I'll learn to fight with every foe
The battle of the Lord.

(*"Thy Word Is Like a Garden, Lord."* Words by Edwin Hodder. Tune: SERAPH. Music by Gottfried W. Fink.)

This chapter is written to help you understand what the Bible is like. It will also give you some ideas on how to use it as the guidebook for your Christian faith and life.

How the Bible Came to Be

The Bible has not always been bound together as one book. It was first written on scrolls made of animal skins. Later it was writ-

ten on papyrus. Papyrus was a tall water plant of the sedge family. Writing material was made from it by soaking, pressing, and drying thin slices of it laid crosswise.

The Bible had been written a long time before it was ever printed by presses and made into the book we know. It was reproduced by hand printing through centuries until after the Middle Ages.

The Bible came gradually into being, book by book, section by section. We are told that before people knew how to write they told parts of it to one another. They passed these stories and thoughts from one generation to another by word of mouth.

Events occurred a long time before they were written. After the events men were led to record them. We believe God inspired people to do the writing. They did not do it on their own. It was done by devout and dedicated people. They were believers and lived close to God. They were a part of God's People, the church. They were inspired by the Spirit of God. To be inspired means "to be breathed into." God's Spirit breathed into the hearts and minds of those who wrote. They were moved and helped to write the truth.

The writing of the Bible covered many centuries. Some say fourteen; others say twenty. This is a long time. People experienced God century after century. They learned much about how God worked. Some believed in God. Some did not. Some obeyed. Some rebelled. This was put into the record.

Some wrote history, like Joshua and Acts. Others recorded the law, like Exodus. Still others composed poetry and songs, like Psalms. Learned and experienced people put together wise sayings, like the Book of Proverbs. The prophets spoke for God. They came to feel God was speaking to them directly. They began their writings with the introduction: "Thus says the Lord." See Isaiah, Jeremiah, and other books of the prophets.

A long period after the Old Testament was completed, the New Testament was put into writing. After Jesus' death and resurrection the Christian Church was born. See Acts 2. Certain men were moved to write the Gospels. About the same time, letters were written by Paul, Peter, and others to Christians and churches. Their purpose was to guide the churches in their faith and life as witnesses of Christ.

Forming the Canon

After the writing a long time passed before the books and letters were accepted. They were not immediately taken as Scripture. Even the writers probably did not know that their words would some day be included in the Bible and regarded as the inspired Word of God.

The word canon means standard. The books of the Bible accepted by the church as being God's Word are referred to as the canon. The process of deciding on these books covered a number of centuries. The church made the final decision on which books were to be included in this list.

There are many books written today about how the Bible came to be. If you are interested you can do further reading about it. See the materials at the end of the chapter. You may find some of them in your church library.

Languages, Translations, and Revisions

The books of the Bible were not written in English. The Old Testament was written in the Hebrew language. The faith it recorded was that of the Hebrews or Jewish people. The New Testament was written in Greek. Greek was the common language spoken in the world at that time. As Christianity moved outward, the Bible was translated into the languages spoken by different races and nations. Later this included the English language.

Hebrew writing looks like this:

בְּרֵאשִׁית בָּרָא אֱלֹהִים אֵת הַשָּׁמַיִם וְאֵת הָאָרֶץ׃

Greek writing looks like this:

For many of us the introduction to the Word of God was through a Bible printed in English. For many years, the most popular English Bible has been the King James Version published in 1611 A.D. In more recent time many new translations have been made from the original languages by groups of scholars. New revisions have also been made. Now we have a variety from which to choose. Around the end of the nineteenth century the American Standard Version was produced. In 1952 the Revised Standard Version was completed. Later came the New English Bible, the Good News Bible (Today's English Version), and others.

Since then we have many more from which to select. The purpose for revisions and translations is to give us a Bible in present-day language so we can understand better what God is saying to us now. Can you name translations other than those we have mentioned?

Some Bibles printed in recent years, like The Living Bible, are paraphrases. They are usually written by an individual, not by a group of biblical scholars. A paraphrase is a rewording of thought and meaning of a writing. Paraphrases do not usually come from a study of ancient manuscripts and original languages.

The Nature of the Bible

There are sixty-six books in the Bible. The word Bible means a collection of writings or books. Thirty-nine books are in the Old Testament. Twenty-seven books are in the New Testament. In the following illustrations the Books are grouped by types of writing such as history, law, etc. The bookcase reminds us that the Bible is a library of different kinds of books.

Try to memorize the books in their proper order. This will help you find passages of Scripture when you are using your Bible. You may wish to ask your teacher for information on the purpose and content of each book. It will also be helpful if you know the meaning of the name of each book. Learn how to spell the names of the books.

The Bible has an Old Testament and a New Testament. The word "testament" means covenant. The church named the two parts of the Bible from the covenants they contain. A covenant is an agreement between two persons, two groups, or a person and a group (like God's covenant with the people of Israel). Each promises to do something.

Old Testament Bookshelf

New Testament Bookshelf

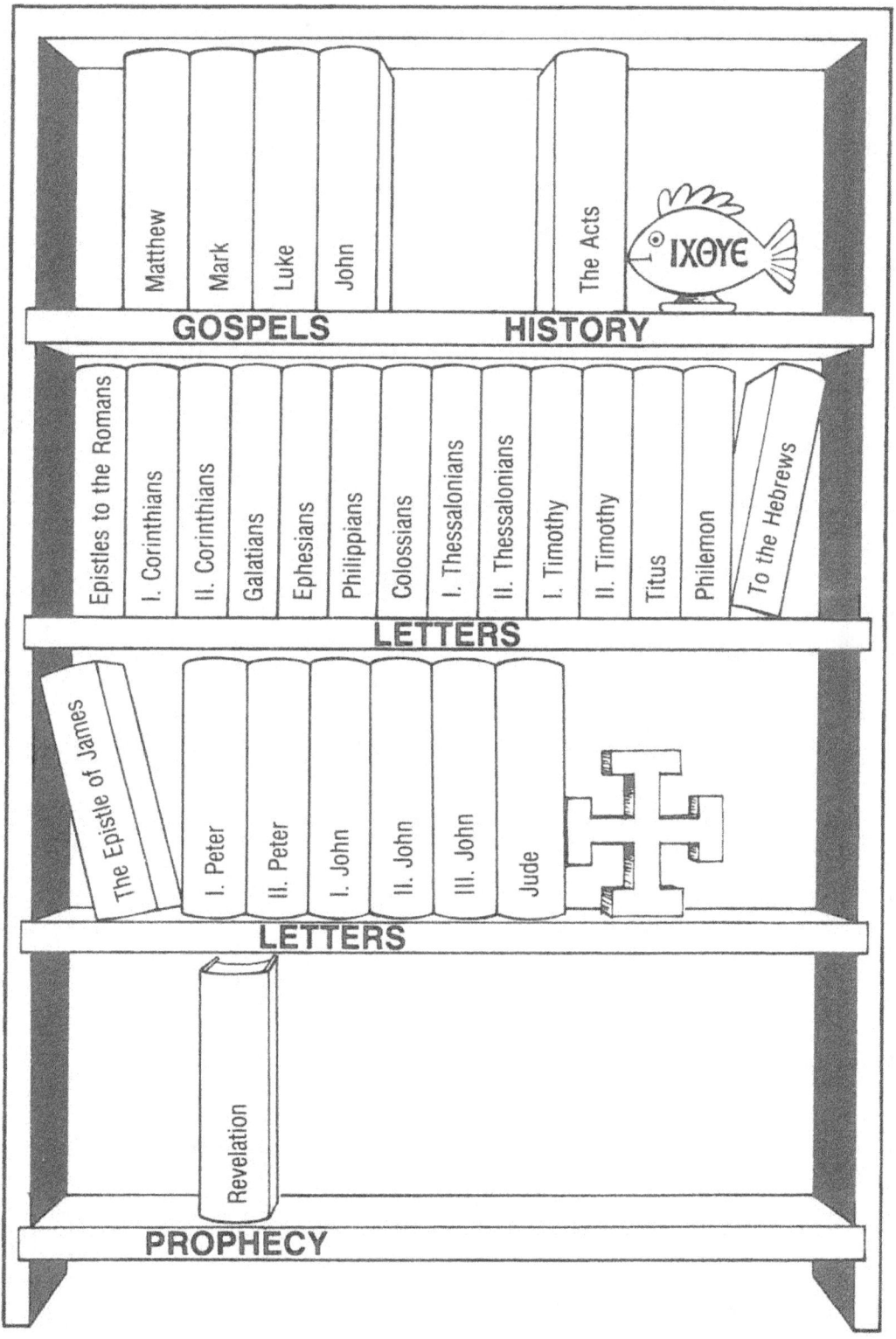

God made the old covenant with the people of Israel at Mount Sinai. He promised to be their God and never to forsake them. They promised to be God's people. The people were to keep the law (which included the Ten Commandments and other laws), as evidence that they were God's people.

Jesus began the new covenant which was made sure by his blood. The sacrifice of Christ was proof of God's love. Our part in the new covenant is trust in and obedience to Jesus Christ as Lord and Savior. But covenants were made between God and the people—not merely between God and one individual. However, we enter into covenant with God one by one or family by family as we own our membership in the church, the covenant community.

Two important words will help you understand further the nature of the Bible. They are revelation and inspiration.

Revelation (rev ′ə-lā ′shən)

Think first of revelation. We believe God loves us and makes God's self known to us. God wants to form a relationship with us. It is something like coming to know another human person. Through sharing we come to know each other better. Revelation is the way in which God moves first to make God's self known to us. This is done in many ways. The Bible is a record of God's revelation of God's self to us.

Here are the ways through which the revelation was made. They are:

1. Objects in the natural world, such as the burning bush from which God spoke to Moses. See Exodus 3:1-4.
2. Events, like the Exodus. The story of God leading the people through the wilderness to the Promised Land is found in the Book of Exodus.
3. Dreams and visions, such as Jacob's dream of the ladder reaching from earth to heaven. See Genesis 28:10-12.
4. Messengers from God, such as the angel speaking to Gideon. See Judges 6:11,12.
5. The voice or word of God, such as God speaking in the Garden of Eden. See Genesis 3:8-13. Also, Jesus speaking to Paul at his conversion. See Acts 9:3-6.
6. Jesus Christ. Through Jesus Christ God showed himself fully and taught us the true nature of life and how it is to be lived. See John 14:7-9; 1:18.
7. The community of the church. God has spoken through the church for centuries. God continues to speak to us when we gather, even in small groups, in Christ's name. See Matthew 18:20.
8. The Holy Spirit. Examples are: Judges 6:34; Acts 2:1-4; John 14:26; Luke 2:25.

We believe God continues to speak to us in many ways. One way is the Scriptures, the only true guide for Christian faith and life.

Inspiration (in ′spə-rā ′shən)

Think now of inspiration. Inspiration is the method by which God oversaw the writing of the Holy Scriptures. The Bible was written by man but the writing was guided by God's Spirit.

The word inspiration comes from the Latin word inspiro which means "breathe into." Inspiration means that God breathed into persons the desire to write and directed them as they wrote. At least three things lead us to believe that the sixty-six books of the Bible have been inspired.

They are:

1. The Bible claims to be inspired. 2 Timothy 3:16.

2. The agreement of the church centuries ago when the canon was closed.

3. The testing of the Bible by life. It has been proved to be a good guide.

You may ask, "How were men inspired? Did God inspire the words, phrases, or thoughts?" First, God inspired men's lives to make them worthy scribes. God inspired their thoughts, rather than inspiring each word and phrase. We reach this conclusion because there are minor differences in the words of the record.

There are different wordings of Jesus' teachings. This is true also for the historical events recorded by the writers of the Gospels. See the different wordings in the two references about the same event given in Matthew 10:5-23 and Mark 6:7-13. The meanings are the same but the words are different.

There are minor differences in reporting the same event, such as Paul's conversion. Read Acts 9, 22, 26.

All such minor differences are of little matter so far as the truth is concerned. The examples above point out that it is not the words that are inspired. If they were, would not all the words be the same for the same teachings and events? It was the general thought and purpose that were inspired. Thoughts, meaning, purpose, and truth in the Bible are all in harmony. There is no disagreement in the Bible about the basic doctrines of our faith.

How to Read and Study the Bible

It is not enough to believe the right things about the Bible. You must learn to read and understand the Bible so it can guide you. Here are some ideas on how to do this:

1. Let the Holy Spirit lead you as you read and study the Bible. Do not read the Bible like any other book. It is not like other books. It was inspired by the Spirit. In order to hear God speak to you from its pages, you must also be guided by the Holy Spirit. Be open to the Spirit as you read it. Know that you need more than your own understanding. You might ask yourself as you read, "What is God saying to me in the Scriptures?"

2. Study the books of the Bible in their historical settings. Everything in the Bible should be understood in the light of the times in which it was written. Consider the conditions under which any passage, book, or letter was written. Know the problems which brought about the writing. Think of the situation to which it speaks.

Find the answers to the questions: Who wrote the book? When was it written? To whom was it written? What was the situation into which it was written? What was being said to the readers? What does the passage say to us?

For practice in studying the Scriptures in their historical settings, find out the background for the letters of Philemon and Philippians.

3. Compare Scripture with Scripture. Each part of the Bible should be seen and understood in the light of the whole book. No part of it should be taken as final by itself. Any passage should be seen in its proper place in the entire record of God's revelation. For instance, if you read James 2:14-16 about good works, you might conclude that God accepts us through our good deeds. If you read also Ephesians 2:8-10, you understand that God accepts us because of our faith, not good deeds. However, we are expected to do good deeds. Another example: If you read Job 14:13-14, you might question the reality of life after death. Read 1 Corinthians 15:20-22 to find an assurance of the resurrection.

4. See the Bible in the light of Jesus Christ. All parts of it are to be understood in view of Jesus Christ's birth, life, teachings, death, and resurrection. He is the very heart of the Bible. God's fullest revelation is made through him. He is the standard by which all biblical writings are to be judged. For example, there are many ideas about what God is like. The Bible reflects different views of God's nature. They range from the idea of a God of anger and judgment to that of a God of love. These views are to be looked at in the light of the question, "What kind of God did Jesus Christ show us?" His word is final. Another example is the commandments. Read the ten commandments in Exodus 20:1-17 and then read what Christ says in Matthew 5:17-47. See the difference.

5. Use the knowledge the church has discovered in the past. There are books which help you understand the Scriptures. They have come out of the life and learning of the church for centuries. These books have insight and wisdom which will inform you concerning the entire Scriptures. Discoveries of old manuscripts and findings from digging in ancient ruins have brought us much knowledge. You need some of this information to help you understand what the Bible is saying. Don't deny yourself the help of this learning. God has been working to give it to us.

6. Share insights with others in the church. The Holy Spirit can speak to you through other church members. Bible study groups provide such an opportunity. You learn much from others as they share knowledge together with you. The Sunday school class provides a setting for such experiences. Studying in groups of two is also a way to additional knowledge. You cannot learn the most from individual Bible study. You cannot depend only on yourself for understanding. You need the church.

Now review these six suggestions. Can you remember them? Read the opening statement of each section. Do this over and over until these ideas stick in your mind. They will be of first importance to you in Bible study.

A Bible Reading Program

An appreciation for the Bible develops through reading it. If you are interested in where to start and the parts of the Bible to start with, you may want to use the following selections over a period of time. You may wish to ask your family to use these for family devotions.

    Creation, Temptation, and Fall: Genesis 1—3
    The Story of Joseph: Genesis 37—50
    The Call of Moses: Exodus 1—4
    The Story of David's Early Years: 1 Samuel 16—20
    Psalms 1, 8, 23, 103, 121
    The Gospel of Mark
    Acts 1—9
    Philippians
    1 and 2 Timothy

Keep a record of your reading in "Log for Journey of Faith."

Jargon for the Journey

BIBLE: The English word comes from biblos, Greek word for books, and biblia, Greek word for collection of writings.

TRANSLATION: The changing of something written from one language to another.

REVISION: The correcting and improving, or bringing up to date, of a translation or a writing.

VERSION: A translation, like the Revised Standard Version of the Bible.

STANDARD: Something (a book or Bible) generally recognized as being excellent and true. Usually approved by some responsible person or organization. King James authorized the translation of the Bible which became the King James Version in 1611 A.D. The translators worked under his authority. The Good News Bible was authorized by the American Bible Society.

MIDDLE AGES: Sometimes called the Dark Ages. A period of European history between 476-1450 A.D.

WITNESS: One who makes his/her faith known by word or deed.

CHAPTER VIII
Christian Worship

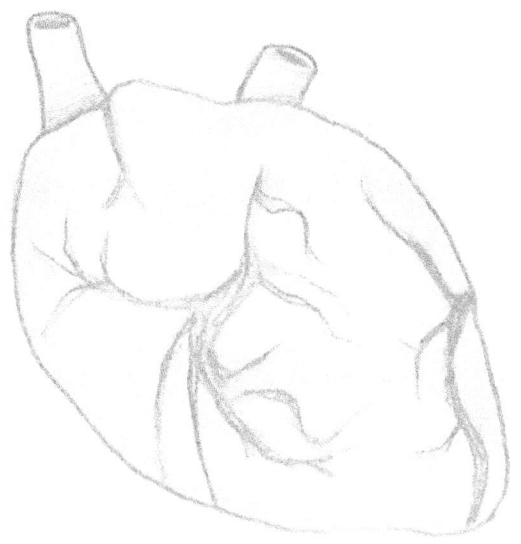

The heart is a good symbol for worship. In the Bible the heart is spoken of as the source of true being. "As he [or she] thinketh in his (her) heart so is he [or she] (Proverbs 23:7, *King James Version*). A good person brings good out of the treasure of good things in his (her) heart . . . For the mouth speaks what the heart is full of." (Luke 6:45, *Good News Bible*). Worship is the response of the heart to God's love. We offer God not only our outward service but our very hearts—purposes, aims, desires, hopes, thoughts—our inner lives.

Christian Worship

"They that worship God must worship God in spirit and in truth." (John 4:24)

Introduction

On your journey of faith, worship is necessary. Some of your earliest memories probably are of going to church. Why do you go?

_____ Because your parents take you
_____ You want to go
_____ To be with friends
_____ To worship God
_____ Other (write in) _____

Check the two major reasons why you go to church.

It is important to have a good reason for attending. If not, going to worship can be a bore or a mere social activity. An understanding of worship will help you find the right reason. This chapter has been written for that purpose.

God, the Center of Worship

The word worship as we use it in this chapter means public worship. Public comes from populus, a Latin word meaning people. Public worship is worship with other people in the congregation. There are other types of worship, such as private, family, and small group. These are important, too.

God is at the center of worship, not we. However, we often let our own needs come first. We may go to church needing forgiveness, encouragement, and help. There is a place in worship for us to bring these needs to God. But they are not to be put first. The purpose of worship is to praise and thank God for what God has already done. It is not only to get something from God. The first question and answer in the Catechism accents this: "What is the chief end of man? Man's chief end is to glorify God and to enjoy him forever." (Catechism, *Confession of Faith*).

Worship Is Praise

The major mark of Christian worship is praise. The pattern is set for us in the New Testament. The early Christians worshiped joyfully. God had saved them from sin to a better life. They rejoiced thankfully in the temple and in their homes. They praised God because they had such good things to share. They ate together, taught each other, and gave gifts. Most of all they celebrated Christ's victory over death which had given them hope.

"And day by day, attending the temple

together and breaking bread in their homes, they partook of food with glad and generous hearts, praising God and having favor with all the people. And the Lord added to their number day by day those who were being saved." (Acts 2:45, 47, *Revised Standard Version*)

". . . be filled with the Spirit, addressing one another in psalms and hymns and spiritual songs, singing and making melody to the Lord with all your heart, always and for everything giving thanks in the name of our Lord Jesus Christ to God the Father." (Ephesians 5:18c-20, *Revised Standard Version*)

The New Testament church was a worshiping community. Its outstanding theme was joyful praise and thanksgiving.

We do not know what their hymns and spiritual songs were. We do know they sang some of the psalms which they had probably used in Jewish worship. These were Psalms 111, 113, 117, 118, 146-50. What are some of the hymns of praise your church sings?

A Model for Worship

The worship of the early Christians is a model for our worship. It is a model not only in spirit and content but in form as well. Given below is a description of their form of worship. You can see how ours is based on theirs.

A Synagogue

The form of early Christian worship came from that in the synagogues. Several centuries before Christ, the people of God were taken into captivity by the Babylonians. The Jewish temple was destroyed. The city of Jerusalem was overrun. The homeland was left in ruins. In Babylon the Jews missed their worship in the temple. They remembered how in the old days people from far and near had come to the temple to worship. They had made sacrifices and heard the great choirs. They had joined gladly in the majestic ceremonies and processions. Now all that had ended.

Historians tell us it was during this time in Babylon that synagogues (meaning "assemblies") were built to fill the need for a place to worship. They were built in the various areas where the Jews had been settled. They were used not only for group worship and private prayer but also for teaching. Schools, especially for instructing the young in the Jewish faith, were held there. In later years when the Jews returned to their homeland, they brought with them the idea of building synagogues in communities where they lived.

The worship was made up of the reading of Old Testament Scriptures, singing, praying, and teaching. Rabbis, the teachers of the Jewish people, spoke on topics of their faith. Since many of the early Christians had been Jews, they carried over into their new faith some of the synagogue forms of worship. They added some parts which came from their Christian faith and teaching. The content of their worship was Christian, not Jewish.

Given below are the things Christians of the first century probably did in their services. Services were held in their homes and in the temple. (The temple had been rebuilt upon the return of the Jews from Babylon many years before.)

—They sang hymns, spiritual songs, and psalms.

"Let the word of Christ dwell in you richly, as you teach and admonish one another in all wisdom, and as you sing psalms and hymns and spiritual songs with thankfulness in your hearts to God." (Colossians 3:16, *Revised Standard Version*).

—They used creeds (statements of what they believed).

It is thought that Scriptures like those below were used as creeds.

"No one can deny how great is the secret of our religion:
He appeared in human form,
was shown to be right by the Spirit,
and was seen by angels.
He was preached among the nations,
was believed in throughout the world,
and was taken up to heaven." (1 Timothy 3:16, *Good News Bible*).

"Have this mind among yourselves, which you have in Christ Jesus, who, though he was in the form of God, did not count equality with God a thing to be grasped, but emptied himself, taking the form of a servant, being born in the likeness of man. And being found in human form he humbled himself and became obedient unto death, even death on a cross. Therefore God has highly exalted him and bestowed on him the name which is above every name, that at the name of Jesus every knee should bow, in heaven and on earth and under the earth, and every tongue confess that Jesus Christ is Lord, to the glory of God the Father." (Philippians 2:5-12, *Revised Standard Version*).

—*They read Scriptures.*
Psalms, the Ten Commandments, and other Old Testament passages were read.
The New Testament had not been written at this time.

—*They prayed.*

—*They broke bread together.*
This was a meal they ate together. We do not know just how it fitted into their service. It was eaten in joy and thanksgiving and so was worshipful in nature.

—*They made gifts to the poor and shared in each others' needs.*

—*They baptized.*

—*Confession of sin.*
Some scholars say that as the life of the church developed, they added:

—*The holy kiss of love* (used in greeting each other). See Romans 16:16; 1 Corinthians 16:20; 2 Corinthians 13:12; 1 Thessalonians 5:26; 1 Peter 5:14.

—*The Lord's Supper* (observed every Lord's day).

—*The Sermon.*

Check the order of worship in your church bulletin. Or, if your church does not have a bulletin, think of the services you have in your church. Are not the parts in the service very similar to those of early Christians? What parts in your church service are the same as those in the early Christian worship? What parts are different? How often does your church celebrate the Lord's Supper?

Worship in Your Congregation

This section of the chapter is written to help you worship in your congregation. We have said praise is the major act of worship. Other acts have a place, too. We list below those acts which make up a complete worship experience. Not all the actions are done by us. God acts also. God says or does something to or for us and we act in response through something we say or do.

God invites us to worship.
We respond by coming.
We praise God.
We confess our sins.
God assures us of forgiveness.
We thank God.
We pray to God.
God speaks to us through the Scriptures.
God speaks to us through the sermon.
God invites us to answer.
We dedicate ourselves to God.
God gives us a blessing.
God sends us back into the world to live as Christians.

These acts are given a place in most worship services. They will make sense as you take part in them. They move forward naturally from one stage to another. Let us see how this works out as we imagine we are going to a service of worship.

We come to worship. We, as a part of God's people, have come to worship. God has called us. This invitation was voiced in a verse of Scripture by the minister. Or it may have been given in his or her own words. The prelude has begun. It marks the beginning of our worship. We become quiet and turn our thoughts toward God. The first prayer recognizes that God meets with us.

We think about ourselves in relation to God. Our lives and salvation come from God. We are sinners who have been saved by Jesus Christ. We live under God's care. Many blessings have come to us this past week. We are now in God's presence, the Creator of the universe and the Giver of life. God is great and loving beyond our knowledge. It is a mystery. We wonder about it. We are touched by God's love shown to us in Jesus Christ.

We praise God. All that God is and has done moves us to praise God. To praise is to express the feeling of God's great worth. It is to lift God up in mind and heart and to voice our highest regard for God. It is to speak of God's greatness and goodness. Through what means

can we express this praise in worship? It is done through singing a hymn such as "Holy, Holy, Holy." It may be done through a responsive or unison reading of Scripture. It may be sung here or in other parts of the service by using the Doxology or the Gloria Patri. The choir may do it for us through an anthem.

We confess our sins. When we recognize how good God is we feel our lack of goodness. We have felt, said, and done things which are wrong. We know we have come short of what we ought to be. We look about us at other worshipers. Together we have all failed. We have done things we ought not to have done. We have left undone things we ought to have done. We are sinners. We confess our sin and ask God to forgive us.

We can make our confession silently. We can do it through singing a hymn like, "Holy Ghost, with Light Divine" or "Jesus, I Come." We may read a printed prayer or a passage of Scripture. We may take part in a litany of confession. (A litany is a prayer which is read or said in turns by the minister and people.)

God assures us of forgiveness. The Scriptures say, "If we confess our sins to God, he will keep his promise and do what is right: he will forgive us our sins and purify us from all wrongdoing." (1 John 1:9, Good News Bible). We depend on the promise of God to forgive when we confess. God offers forgiveness to us right now. In faith and trust we accept the forgiveness God offers. We feel relief, gratitude, and peace. The assurance of forgiveness may be put into words by the minister as a suitable verse of Scripture is read after our confession. The choir or congregation may sing a line or two of a hymn like "Blessed Assurance" or "Just As I Am." The choir may sing an anthem like "God So Loved the World."

We thank God. Our joy over being forgiven moves us to give thanks to God. We cannot forgive ourselves. Only God can forgive. Forgiveness flows freely when we ask. Now we express our gratitude as completely as we can. We cannot say enough to match the gift. We think also of other gifts God has given us: home, family, friends, food, clothing, minds, bodies, churches, the wonderful world and the universe. We are moved to want to give something in return to show our thanks.

Gladly we give thanks through a hymn like "For the Beauty of the Earth" or "O for a Thousand Tongues." We may do it through a silent prayer. Some of the Psalms are good means of saying thanks. Or during the offering we may make a gift of money as an act of thanksgiving.

We pray to God. The service of worship may include a number of shorter prayers. They are the invocation, the adoration, dedication of offering, and the prayer before the sermon. It may include a longer prayer by the minister. This prayer is sometimes called the morning prayer or the pastoral prayer. It includes praise, confession, and thanksgiving. Prayer is usually made for the ill, the troubled, and the sorrowful. Other concerns may be the whole church, the nation, and the world. In this prayer the minister speaks for the congregation. That is, the minister is saying the prayer in our place or for us. Our part is to listen and to join silently in the praying. We do this also for other prayers. The times of prayer give us a chance for direct sharing with God. We may be able to experience God in this way at church more than at any other time of the week.

God speaks to us through the Scriptures. We believe the Bible is the Word of God, a true guide for our living. Through its pages God speaks to us. Special passages are usually read

every Sunday. As they are being read we listen for God's Word to us. We shut out other thoughts. We may find some passages easy to understand. Others will bring questions. We do our best to get the meaning. We may ask as the Word is being read, "How does this apply to me?"

God speaks to us through the sermon. God continues to speak to us through the minister. The minister explains the Scriptures and tells us what they say about our lives. We do our best to listen. What is being said is important to us as Christians. If we listen well we can hear something that helps us. The sermon may also touch our hearts to make us want to be better people.

God invites us to answer. God invites us to answer the call to obey and the offer of love given in the sermon. The invitation is given by the minister. We may be asked to become Christians or to take forward steps in our Christian living.

We dedicate ourselves to God. We answer God's invitation in some way. Our worship is not complete unless we do. We may decide to accept and to follow Jesus Christ. We may decide to right some wrong in our lives; to serve someone in need; to begin to love God more; to give our lives more completely to God's will. Or we may simply say, "God, I want to be better. Help me."

There are several ways we can dedicate ourselves. We can go to the minister and make our aim known to everyone. We can sing a hymn of dedication such as "Take My Life, and Let it Be Consecrated, Lord, to Thee." We may make an offering. We may recite a statement of faith with the congregation like the Apostles' Creed.

God gives us a blessing. At the close of the service God gives us a blessing. It is given to us in the scriptural benediction or closing prayer by the minister. We receive it gratefully as coming directly from God. An example of a biblical benediction is "The grace of the Lord Jesus Christ, the love of God, and the fellowship of the Holy Spirit be with you all." (2 Corinthians 13:13, *Good News Bible*).

God sends us back into the world to live as Christians. God sends us out into the world with a blessing. We return to live as Christians, made stronger by having worshiped. God goes with us. We are not alone.

Your experience of worship may or may not be exactly like that described above. It is possible for you to worship in more than one way. The acts of worship as described, however, make up a complete worship experience. They are a dependable guide. Keep them in mind to help you understand what you do when you go to church. You may also find help by talking your worship over with your minister.

Worship and Life

The things we have said above are important in worship. There is something which is even more important. It is connecting our worship with our living.

Christian worship and Christian living belong together. We cannot separate them. Worship is incomplete if it ends in the actual worship period. It must reach into life and affect our living. A poet has said that the truest worship is noble deeds. Worship and life should be blended together.

O brother man, fold to thy heart thy brother;
Where pity dwells, the peace of God is there;
To worship rightly is to love each other,
Each smile a hymn, each kindly deed a prayer.

For he whom Jesus loved has truly spoken:
The holier worship which He deigns to bless
Restores the lost, and binds the spirit broken,
And feeds the widow and the fatherless.

Follow with reverent steps the great example
Of Him whose holy work was doing good;
So shall the wide earth seem our Father's temple,
Each loving life a psalm of gratitude.
—*John Greenleaf Whittier*

Our *Confession of Faith* (1883), Section 77, names those acts which are considered proper worship. They include ". . . visiting the sick, contributing to the relief of the poor, and the support and spread of the gospel . . ." Our church has taught for a long time that worship is to be a part of our living.

We are taught in the Bible to make worship and life parts of a whole response to God's love. Here are some examples:

To be right with God we must be right with our brothers and sisters. "So if you are about to offer your gift to God at the altar and there you remember that your brother has something against you, leave your gift there in front of the altar, go at once and make peace with your brother, then come back and offer your gift to God." (Matthew 5:23-24, *Good News Bible*).

We must not only worship, we must obey. "Why do you call me 'Lord, Lord,' and yet don't do what I tell you?" (Luke 6:46, *Good News Bible*).

We must not only receive Christ's love in worship at church; we must give love to others out in the world every day. "This is how we know what love is: Christ gave his life for us. We too, then, ought to give our lives for our brothers! If a rich person sees his brother in need, yet closes his heart against his brother, how can he claim that he loves God? My children, our love should not be just words and talk, it must be true love, which shows itself in action." (1 John 3:16-18, *Good News Bible*).

We can't say we love God unless we love our brothers and sisters. "If someone says he loves God, but hates his brother, he is a liar. For he cannot love God, whom he has not seen, if he does not love his brother, whom he has seen. The command that Christ has given us is this: whoever loves God must love his brother also. (1 John 4:20, 21, *Good News Bible*).

The Sacraments—An Introduction

Worship through the sacraments will be discussed in Chapters 9 and 10. They are a part of a complete worship experience, though in our churches they are not celebrated every Sunday.

A sacrament is a symbol that represents something else. Symbols can be pictures, designs, colors, acts, monograms (initials), marks, or words. Examples are: A handshake represents and expresses friendship. A kiss represents and expresses affection and love. A wave of the hand represents the recognition of a friend. A cross represents the death of Christ.

We generally use the word sacrament to refer to baptism and the Lord's Supper which were approved by Jesus. These sacraments are symbols of God's love given to us freely. Through them God actively expresses love to us. By celebrating the sacraments we respond to that love.

Sacraments are to be celebrated. To celebrate is to mark an event with joy. It is to rejoice with others in happy thanksgiving for God's gifts. It is to remember and to dedicate. You will hear such terms as administering the sacraments, observing the sacraments, receiving the sacraments. The most meaningful one is celebrating the sacraments. This is the term we will use more than the others.

These thoughts will be more fully developed in the next two chapters.

A Suggested Activity

In "Log for Journey of Faith," record the answers to at least two of the questions below.

1. Recall an experience you have had at church which you regard as worship. What did you think? feel? do? Do you have these experiences often?

2. The next time you go to church, try this: Jot down how you felt during the service. List where the acts of worship fitted into your service. How were the people of different ages included?

3. How are symbols used in your worship? Do they help you to worship better? Your church probably has some symbols in it. See how many you can find in your church. List them and ask yourself how you can use them to improve your worship.

a. What symbolic colors are in your church? (Like white for purity, green for life and growth, purple for royalty, red for sacrifice.)

b. Are there any pictures?

c. What symbolic objects do you have? (Like the cross for Christ's death, two candles on the altar for Christ's human-divine nature.)

d. Are there any monograms (initials) of Greek words for Christ? (Like IHS [Jesus] and XP [Christ].)

e. What does the fire on the lighted candles stand for?

f. Do you have art glass (cathedral) windows with symbols? Are the windows gothic (pointed at the top)? What is the symbol of a gothic window?

g. What symbolic acts are done in your church? (Like bowing in reverence for prayer, standing in honor and praise of God, kneeling in humility.)

Our Christian Symbols, Friedrich Rest, Christian Education Press, and *Symbols of the Faith,* Warner L. Hall, CLC Press, are small books which will help you understand and use symbols.

4. What do you do to prepare yourself for worship on Sunday?

5. In your situation, what can you do to relate worship to life?

CHAPTER IX
The Sacrament of Baptism

The descending dove is the symbol for baptism. It is the sign of the coming of the Holy Spirit into our lives.

The Sacrament of Baptism

Jerry had gone to church with his parents. Like other boys and girls, he sat with a group of his own age. At the close of the service something very unusual happened. Jerry and the others really paid attention.

After the sermon the minister, Jenny Howard, gave an invitation. She asked any who wished to profess their faith in Jesus Christ to come to the front.

Two people came. One was Joe Houston, a grandfather in his seventies. The other was Howie Johnson, his grandson, about twelve. They were part of a family who had moved to town last year. Jerry was in school with Howie.

Ms. Howard said she had discussed the church with Mr. Houston and Howie and their family. They wanted to profess their faith and take the church covenant.

Mr. Houston had never been a Christian. He had let the years go by without taking this important step. He had never been baptized. Howie's mother and father were church members. They had had him baptized when he was a baby.

Howie and his grandfather answered the questions in the church covenant together. It was quite an experience for everyone. A grandfather and a grandson commiting themselves to the church at the same time!

After the questions were answered the Reverend Ms. Howard said, "Mr. Houston, we have discussed the meaning of baptism. Are you ready to receive the sacrament?" He said, "I am." The congregation watched with interest and joy as the pastor baptized Mr. Houston. The pastor then turned to Howie and said, "Howie, you were baptized when you were a baby. We have discussed what that meant. Do you accept the baptism you received then?" Howie looked at his parents and said, "I do."

The minister prayed. The benediction was given. The people were invited to come welcome these two newest members of the church.

How do you think Mr. Houston felt during this service? What had the minister told him about baptism? How do you think Howie felt? How did Howie's parents feel about it all? What had Howie been taught about the meaning of his baptism as a child? You will find the answers in this chapter.

This chapter tells about the basic meaning of baptism. It will also include the special meaning of baptism for a child of believing parents.

Two Ways of Baptizing

There are two ways baptism is done. One is by immersion, which is dipping or putting the whole body of a person under water. The other is by pouring or sprinkling water upon a person's head. Our *Confession of Faith* states that sprinkling or pouring is the accepted way of baptism for our church, but that its meaning does not depend on how it is done.

Usually in celebrating the sacrament of baptism in our church, water is poured or sprinkled upon the person's head. The minister says, "I baptize you in the name of the Father and of the Son and of the Holy Spirit." This act symbolizes the coming of the Holy Spirit into our hearts and lives. It is a sign that those receiving baptism are taking the name of God upon themselves and are sharing in God's nature. Although our church generally practices sprinkling or pouring, if those who have been immersed wish to join one of our congregations, their baptism is accepted.

Baptism by immersion symbolizes the death, burial, and resurrection of Jesus Christ. It also symbolizes that the person being baptized is dying to sin, being buried with Christ in baptism, and rising with him to new life. Note that in each action the way of baptism symbolizes something different. Each way of baptism fits what it symbolizes.

Have you ever wondered why water is used for baptism? People have always used water to wash dirt off their bodies and to keep them clean. This suggests the reason water is used for baptism. It is a symbol for being made clean of sin. It is a sign of being made pure. "I will sprinkle clean water on you and make you clean from all your idols and everything else that has defiled you." (Ezekiel 36:25, *Good News Bible*).

Water is used in baptism for another reason. Baptism was begun in a land where water was scarce. Life depends on water. To use water as a religious symbol was to confess dependence on God who supplies daily needs. To receive baptism is to confess that we depend on God for all that is necessary for our salvation.

If you profess faith in Jesus Christ and enter into the church covenant but have never been baptized, the minister baptizes you. Through this sacrament God says, "I love and accept you in Jesus Christ. I forgive your sins and give you eternal life. I set you apart from the world to serve and follow Christ." The water sprinkled on your head is the outward symbol of this experience. It is a sign of membership in the covenant community.

If you profess faith in Jesus Christ and enter into the church and were baptized as a baby, the minister asks, "Do you accept the baptism you received as a child?" You answer, "I do." In accepting your baptism you may also experience assurance of God's love and your commitment to Christ.

Baptism Is Not the Means of Salvation

Although our salvation is marked by baptism, baptism does not save us. We are saved by faith in Jesus Christ. Baptism is the sign of our salvation. Although it is only a symbol, it is important. It has many meanings for us.

The Meanings of Baptism

In baptism God speaks and acts. The sacraments are gifts from God. Through the gift of baptism God says something to us. It is like your saying something to a friend by a gift. If you give a friend a ring or a bracelet you are saying, "I like you. I am your friend." In the gift of baptism God says, "I love and accept you in Jesus Christ." God says this through the Holy Spirit, the minister, and the baptism.

God also acts in and through baptism. God touches you through the water put on your head. God is present in the words and acts of the sacrament. God is present in those about you loving you through them. This is true when you are baptized as a baby. It affects you though you may not understand how. It is true when you are baptized as a youth or adult. You can know it through your faith.

In a Lutheran congregation the children had come to the kneeling rail at the front of the church. People were celebrating the Lord's Supper. The children did not receive the bread and wine. Instead, the minister marked the cross on their forehead with his finger and said, "Remember your baptism."

This is a helpful word to us: "Remember your baptism." Once baptized, remember it. Call it to mind from time to time. It is a sign of God's love. Just like the wedding ring reminds married partners of each other's love. So you won't forget God's love, remember your baptism. So you won't forget that you have been set apart to follow Christ, remember your baptism.

Baptism is the symbol of the coming of the Holy Spirit into your life. (See the symbol of the descending dove.) It is a symbol of your being born of the Spirit. Jesus said, "A person is born physically of human parents, but he is born spiritually of the Spirit. Do not be surprised because I tell you that you must all be born again." (John 3:6,7, *Good News Bible*).

Your experience of being born of the Spirit will be your own. It may happen in one way or another. On the one hand, you may sense God's call and respond. You may feel God coming into your heart. You are touched emotionally. You may or may not shed tears. You say you believe in Jesus Christ. You take him as your Lord and Savior. It is an experience which you will not forget.

On the other hand, you may not have such a definite experience. You may come to know that God is already in your life. You belong to God. God is real to you. You may not remember when this happened. You know it to be true. You may have always felt this way.

James said, "The wind blows wherever it wishes; you hear the sound it makes, but you do not know where it comes from or where it is going. It is like that with everyone who is born of the Spirit." (John 3:8, *Good News Bible*). The Spirit comes as the wind. It is a mystery. Wind comes as a gentle breeze, a strong gale, or a great storm. It comes in different ways. None of us has the same experience, but we can all know the same Spirit.

When you are born again, the Holy Spirit is present in your life. In being baptized you act out this fact. Water is sprinkled on your head. Remember your baptism. It will help you be more sure that you have been born of the Spirit.

Baptism is a symbol of your belonging to the church. You belong. You belong like you belong to your family. Like you belong in your home. It is a part of your life and you are part of it. You belong together.

Through baptism you are set apart as belonging to God and God's people. Through it you have taken a new step. You have crossed a line. You are no longer outside but inside. You no longer belong to yourself but to God and the church. You belong to that great company of people who bear the name of Christ. Some of them are dead but live in heaven. Some live today all around the earth. Others are yet to be born.

Remember your baptism. It tells everyone to whom you belong. One day Susan, an eleven-year-old girl, was baptized. Some of her friends who were not church members asked her what it meant. Her father was a rancher. She had seen him and his workers brand cattle. Susan said to her friends, "God has put his brand on me." You do this sometimes with a pet. You get a tag or a license and attach it to a collar. You put it on your cat or dog. Everyone knows who owns it. So in baptism God marks you. Through it you tell everyone you belong to God and God's people. What a joy to belong! To be inside and not outside. To be part of God and God's household.

Baptism sets you apart for service. Through baptism you bear the mark of Christ. Your life is no longer your own. It belongs to him. It is to be used in his work. You are yoked with him and will learn how to serve. All Christians are yoked together with him. They learn to serve together from him.

This figure of the yoke comes from the New Testament. "Take my yoke and put it on you, and learn from me, because I am gentle and humble in spirit; and you will find rest." (Matthew 11:29, *Good News Bible*). Have you ever seen an ox yoke? In New Testament times people used oxen as their work animals. Life was largely rural. Farming was the main vocation. Usually two oxen were yoked together. A large wooden beam carved to fit the shoulders of the animals was placed across their necks. It was four or five feet long and at least four to six inches thick. It was held to the shoulders by oxbows. These were curved pieces of wood made of small trees or branches placed under and around the necks of the animals and connected to the yoke. Ropes or chains were tied to the yoke and attached to the plow or cart which the oxen were to pull.

When a farmer needed to break in or train a young ox to work, he yoked it with an older, more experienced ox. The young animal learned from the older. So with Christ and us. We are yoked with him in baptism. From him we learn together to love and serve. As we work we also learn from each other.

Review

Can you remember these four meanings of baptism that have been named?

1. In baptism God speaks and acts.
2. Baptism is the symbol of the coming of the Holy Spirit into human life.
3. Baptism is a symbol of belonging to the church.
4. Baptism sets a person apart for service.

Baptism of a Child

Baptism has the same basic meanings for everyone. Baptism of a child has some special meanings. Were you baptized as a baby? When? Where? By whom? How were you dressed? What have your parents told you about the event? Discuss your baptism with your family.

The following paragraphs will help you think about the special meaning of baptism for a child of believing parents. Children of nonbelievers are not to be presented for baptism. The reasons for this will become clear as you read further.

What Baptism of a Child Is Not

It is not a christening. A christening is usually thought of as being the dedication of a child. Like baptism, christening includes the giving of a name to the child. Baptism has a much broader meaning than christening. You will see this as you read the next pages.

Baptism does not give the child salvation. Salvation comes through faith in Jesus Christ. Baptism does not take from the child the right of deciding for one's self whether to become a Christian. Later the child will be given the opportunity to respond to the inner call to accept Jesus Christ.

Baptism is not to be done in private. It is to be done in the congregation. It is not a private sacrament. It is for the whole church. Sometimes parents mistakenly request that it be done in their home or a chapel with only members of the family present. To do this denies the true nature of the sacrament.

You may be asking, "Well, what does it mean? Where is it to be done? Why does our church baptize children? Here are some answers:

Biblical Reasons for Baptizing a Child

There are biblical reasons for believing in and practicing the baptism of children.

First, when God made the covenant with Abraham children were included. Read Genesis 17:7. According to the New Testament, children are still included in the covenant community when their parents become members. Read Acts 2:39.

Second, in the New Testament, when the head of the home became Christian and was baptized, all members of the household were baptized. This marked them as a Christian family. Doubtless, children were included. Read Acts 16:15, about the baptism of Lydia; and Acts 16:33, about the baptism of the jailer.

Third, in 1 Corinthians 7:14, Paul wrote

that even one believing parent makes the children acceptable to God. Acceptable means they belong to God. They are acceptable to be a part of God's people. They are acceptable because of their relation to the believing parent. If you are born of a citizen of the United States, you are a United States citizen. In the same way, if you are born of a member of the household of faith, you are a member of the household of faith. This is because of your family relationship. Later, you can make it your own by choice.

Fourth, Jesus taught that children in their innocence are members of the kingdom. Read Matthew 18:1-5 and 19:14. Since this is true, we believe children are entitled to receive the sacrament of baptism.

Fifth, Jesus invited children to come to him. He loved and accepted them. We believe he still invites them to come and he receives them as they are. Read Matthew 19:13-15; Mark 10:13-16; Luke 18:16,17.

Meanings of Baptism of a Child

There are great meanings for those who celebrate the sacrament of baptism of a child. Never make light of it. It is an event of great joy. Parents and other members of the church are often led to feel God's presence as the baby is presented for baptism. Tears of happiness

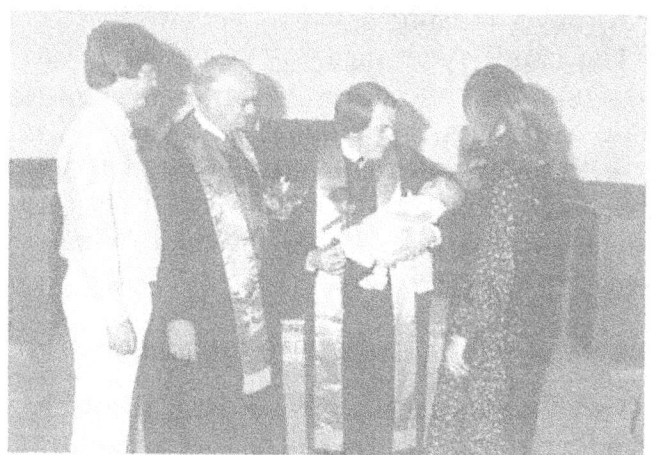

are sometimes shed. Smiles of approval are given. It is a time of true worship as the congregation shares this important happening with the family.

Special meanings of the event include the following:

The sacrament is a symbol of the child's belonging in the church. When a child is baptized in the congregation the parent or parents and the people are saying through the sacrament, "This child is a member of the church."

When you were born, if one or both parents were church members, you were a member, too. You belonged in the church because of their belonging. You were a member from the very moment of your birth. You were born into the church.

If you were baptized your name was written into the church roll as a child member. (You may ask the clerk of the session to show you your name on the church roll.) The baptism did not make you a part of the church. It recognized that you already were a part of it because of your family. This is true for all children born in a Christian home.

This has not taken away your right to decide for yourself. You may have already made the decision or will make it. Until you do you are a member through your family. When you do decide you will be a member through your own choice. You will continue to belong.

Through the sacrament parents accept the offer of God's love for themselves and their child. If you were baptized as a baby, one or both of your parents were church members. They had accepted the covenant of grace. They had taken the church covenant. At your baptism they accepted the covenant again. They promised again to believe and to be faithful church members. But they took one more very big step. They accepted the covenant of grace for you. They promised to answer to God for you. They said they would rear you as a Christian; teach you what it means to believe; answer for you until you could answer for yourself. They said they would guide, instruct, and correct you. Just as they would feed you food for your body, they would feed you spiritually to help you grow in faith. This was a big promise. They answered to God for you. Someday they hoped you would answer for yourself. They believed you would.

Through the sacrament the congregation promises to aid the parents. If you were baptized as a baby, your parents knew they needed help to carry out their promises. They could not do it on their own. They asked for God's help then and many times later. They also needed the help of the congregation.

The congregation could supply Christian teaching and Bible study by good teachers. It could provide a fellowship with many ages and groups of people who would be of help to you as you grew up. An atmosphere of love and caring would be the source of strength. The pastor through visits in the home, sermons, and loving care would be a source of encouragement.

Usually at the baptism of a child the minister in charge asks the congregation if they will help the parents. The people say, "We will." Your parents probably felt encouraged when the congregation promised to help them. There are many ways in which the congregation has helped you grow in your faith.

The sacrament of baptism is never to be repeated. If you were baptized as a child, and want to become a committed church member, you will be asked to accept the baptism you received then. The minister will probably remind you what baptism means. He or she may recall that your parents were faithful in having you baptized as a child. Your baptism may have meaning for you because your parents taught you about it.

Baptism Is a Part of Worship

The sacrament of baptism for a child is celebrated as a part of the worship of the congregation. The congregation gathers for worship. The service is begun. At a fitting time the sacrament is celebrated in the following or similar manner:

The minister will stand near the baptismal font or a table on which a baptismal cup is placed. He or she invites the parent or parents to present the child. Sometimes the grandparents and other members of the family are invited to come with them. The minister announces who is presenting their child.

He or she may say a few words about the meaning of the sacrament.

The parents are asked if they confess their faith in Christ and if they will teach the faith to the child. They answer, "We do and we will."

The congregation is asked if they will work with the family in teaching the child. They answer, "We will."

The child is taken into the arms of the minister. (Sometimes the parents continue to hold the child for the baptism.)

The minister asks the name of the child, then calling the child's name, sprinkles water on the child's head, saying, "_____, I baptize you in the name of the Father, and of the Son, and of the Holy Spirit."

A prayer is said.

The child is returned to the parents, who may take the child to the nursery or keep the child with them in worship.

A fitting hymn may be sung by the congregation, like "Jesus Loves Me," "Tell Me the Stories of Jesus," or "I Think When I Read that Sweet Story."

What If the Child Is Not Baptized?

Perhaps the question has arisen about the standing of a child who has not been baptized. Here are some ideas which may be of help.

A long time ago our church said it believed that all babies and young children were accepted by God. If any of them should die they are saved through Christ. We believe that all children come from God and belong to God.

Many parents in the world do not recognize this. They do not enter into the covenant with God. They do not teach their children of God's love. In spite of this, God loves them. God will call them and move them toward Christ. God calls everyone. All children will be given an opportunity to accept salvation when they grow up and are able to answer for themselves.

If your parents did not have you baptized as a baby, you may wonder why. Discuss this fact with them. Remember that baptism does not save you. If your parents are in the covenant community, you have been included in that covenant, whether you are baptized or not. We do not want you to be hurt or worried over the matter. Don't let it prevent you from professing faith in Jesus Christ and becoming a committed member of the church. If you have not been baptized, you will receive baptism when you join the church.

Some Things to Do

(1) Why is the dove used as a symbol of baptism? Read Matthew 3:16 and John 1:32. Record these verses in "Log for Journey of Faith."

(2) Talk to your parents about your baptism and what it meant to them. If you were not baptized, talk this over with your parents.

(3) Observe the baptism of a child. How was it done? What questions were asked? What did the minister say and do?

(4) Interview the minister and ask him or her how he or she baptizes a child.

Jargon for the Journey

GRACE: The love God gives us which we can never deserve. God's influence acting in us to lead us to holy living. The condition of a person thus influenced. The covenant of grace is God's promise of love and God's acceptance of us.

CELEBRATE: To mark an event with joy. It involves remembering, giving thanks, and dedicating or rededicating ourselves.

IMMERSION: The act of baptizing a person by dipping or putting the whole body under water.

POURING OR SPRINKLING: The act of baptizing a person by putting water upon his or her head.

SALVATION: Being brought into right relationship with God and others through faith in Jesus Christ.

COVENANT COMMUNITY: The covenant community is the people of God, the church.

CHURCH COVENANT: The questions which are asked when persons are being received into church membership. They are answered by "I do" or "I will."

CHAPTER X
The Sacrament of the Lord's Supper

The loaf and the cup are symbols for the sacrament of the Lord's Supper. Christ's body was broken and Christ's blood was shed for us. He is the bread of life for strength. He is the source of life and power for service.

The Sacrament of the Lord's Supper

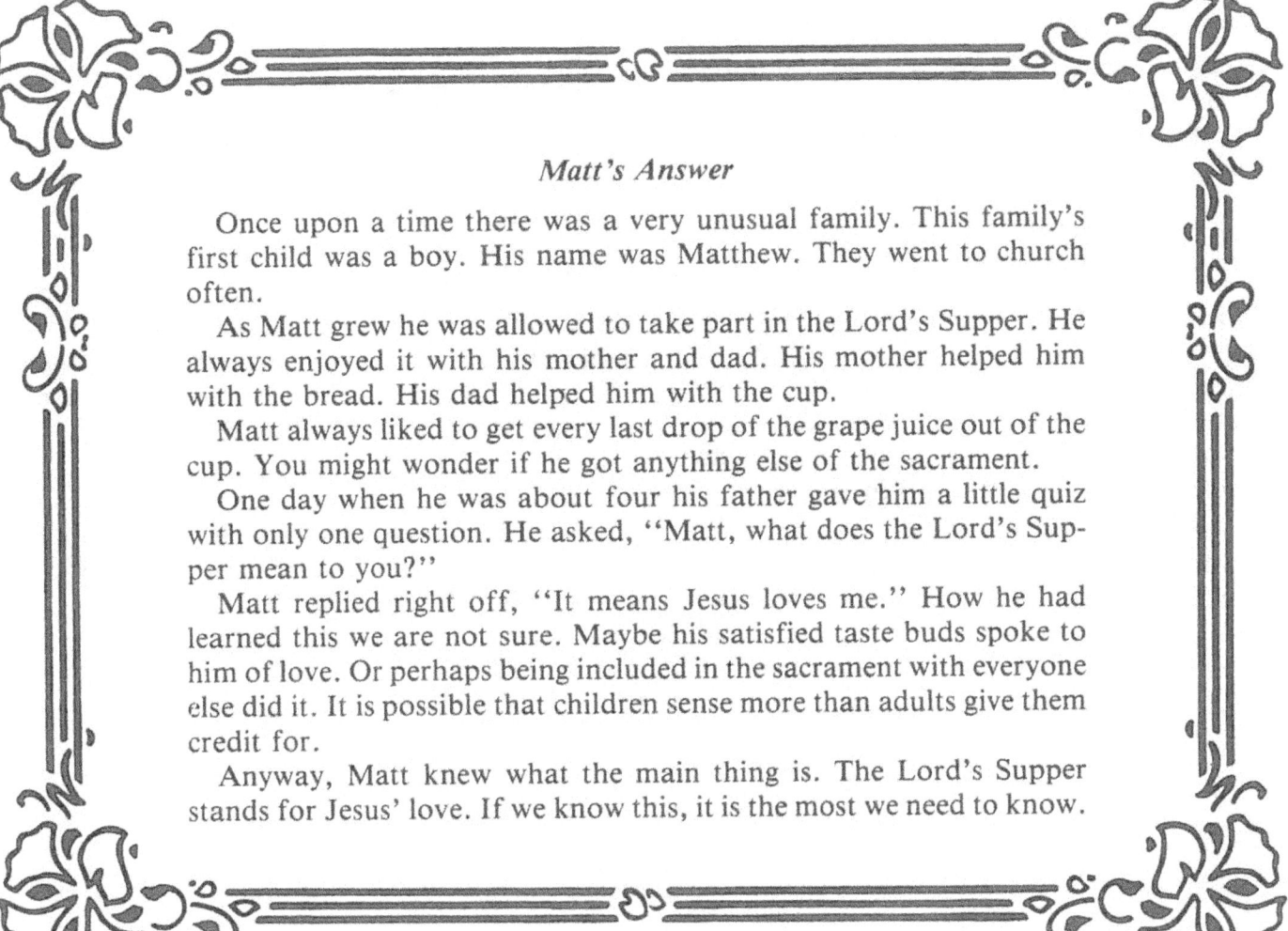

Matt's Answer

Once upon a time there was a very unusual family. This family's first child was a boy. His name was Matthew. They went to church often.

As Matt grew he was allowed to take part in the Lord's Supper. He always enjoyed it with his mother and dad. His mother helped him with the bread. His dad helped him with the cup.

Matt always liked to get every last drop of the grape juice out of the cup. You might wonder if he got anything else of the sacrament.

One day when he was about four his father gave him a little quiz with only one question. He asked, "Matt, what does the Lord's Supper mean to you?"

Matt replied right off, "It means Jesus loves me." How he had learned this we are not sure. Maybe his satisfied taste buds spoke to him of love. Or perhaps being included in the sacrament with everyone else did it. It is possible that children sense more than adults give them credit for.

Anyway, Matt knew what the main thing is. The Lord's Supper stands for Jesus' love. If we know this, it is the most we need to know.

Keep this story in mind as you read this chapter. It will help you see the main meaning of the Lord's supper.

The Beginning of the Lord's Supper

The Lord's Supper was first celebrated at night. Jesus and his disciples had met together in a large upstairs room in Jerusalem. After their meal Jesus took a piece of bread. He gave thanks and broke it. He gave it to the disciples and said: "This is my body which is broken for you. Do this in remembrance of me." He also took a cup and said: "This cup is the new covenant in my blood. Do this, as often as you drink it, in remembrance of me." (Read 1 Corinthians 11:23-26, *Revised Standard Version,* and Mark 14:15, *Good News Bible.*)

Early in the first century, Christians began to celebrate this sacrament when they met together. It was done in company with other believers. It has continued as a sacrament of the church.

In Cumberland Presbyterian congregations, the Lord's Supper is under the direction of the church session. The minister and elders preside over it. Usually the elders serve the elements (bread and wine) to the congregation. Most of our congregations use unfermented grape juice rather than wine.

The Lord's Supper is celebrated in a service

of worship. Usually the first part of the worship includes a sermon. The second part includes the sacrament.

Some people speak of receiving the sacrament, administering the sacrament, and observing the sacrament. We will use celebrating the sacrament. To celebrate is to mark an event with joy, to remember, give thanks, and dedicate.

Names of the Sacrament

Several names are used for this sacrament.

The *Lord's Supper* is perhaps the most often used and best known name. It came from the fact that Jesus' last meal with the disciples was a supper. This title will be used more than others in these pages. Jesus is the host. He has invited his friends to come. Eating together is a symbol of love and acceptance.

The *holy communion* may have been used from the earliest days of the church. Communion means spiritual fellowship. It suggests that in the supper we share deeply together with Christ. "The cup we use in the Lord's Supper and for which we give thanks to God: when we drink from it, we are sharing in the blood of Christ. And the bread we break: when we eat it, we are sharing in the body of Christ." (1 Corinthians 10:16, *Good News Bible.*)

The *eucharist* (u'k-rist) is the Greek word for thanksgiving. Some churches use only this name. It refers to Christ's giving thanks when he broke the bread and poured the wine. This name suggests that the sacrament is a feast of thanks for God's gift of his son.

The *sacrament* is often used. It comes from the Latin word sacramentum, which was an oath of loyalty made each year by a roman soldier to his emperor. The early church made it into a Christian word. Through the sacrament we promise to be faithful to Christ and the church.

The *mass* is another name for the Lord's Supper. It is used in Orthodox and Roman Catholic churches. Its beginning is interesting. In the fourth and fifth centuries worship in

Christian churches was divided into two parts. The first was open to everyone. It included Bible reading, singing, prayer, and a sermon. When this part of the service was over, the public was dismissed. The minister said, "Ite

missa est" (go; you are dismissed) or simply "Missa" (dismissed). Only baptized members were welcome to the second part of the service. It was mainly the Lord's Supper. Missa or mass, which was used to signal the end of the public worship, came to stand for the sacrament. (See *Meditations for Communion Services,* William Latane Lumpkin, Abingdon, pp. 40, 41.)

Mass is not used in Cumberland Presbyterian churches. It suggests meanings for the Lord's Supper different from our beliefs. Those who use it believe Christ is sacrificed again at each mass. We believe Christ's sacrifice was made once on the cross. We celebrate this act of love in the Lord's Supper.

Meanings in the Lord's Supper

If you were asked what the Lord's Supper means to you, what would you say? Take time to think about this question. State aloud or write down one or more answers you would give.

The names given above suggest some meanings. Seeing the Lord's Supper celebrated has taught you something about it. If you have taken part in the sacrament you have still more understanding.

Would you like to know more? If so, read the following short story. Does it give some hints of the meanings? If so, what are they?

A Story: A Symbol of Friendship

Scott and Chris were good friends. They were both twelve years of age. Scott was a few months older and larger than Chris. Their families were very much alike. The fathers worked for large companies. They moved from one place to another every few years because of their work. The mothers helped everyone adjust to each move. Sometimes they worked away from home, too.

Both families had lived in several states. They had been in Huntsville, Alabama, now for nearly three years. Their homes were in the same block. The boys spent many hours together.

They shared many interests. Both liked sports. Both loved music. They enjoyed hiking through the country. They explored new places. Each dared the other to do risky things.

They were full of life and noisy. They often "broke out in all directions." Their grades were average. Sometimes they called attention to themselves in school.

They also found time for serious talks about life and what they would do someday. They encouraged each other. They were very special friends. They enjoyed being together.

One day a very sad thing happened. Scott's father got word from his company that he was to leave Huntsville. He was being sent overseas for at least three years. The family would go with him. They had three weeks to get ready.

The boys were really upset. They were mad and sad at the same time. Three years they had shared everything. Now they had to separate. All they were doing and planned to do would be changed. What could they do to keep in touch?

Why not give each other a special gift? But what would it be? What did each like? How could they please each other? They were very open in talking about it.

Finally they decided what they would do. Each would give the other a ring. The gifts would be signet rings with an initial on the set of each one. C for Chris. S for Scott. But the

rings would be switched. Chris would wear the one with the S and Scott would wear the one with the C. Each would be reminded of the other. It was a sort of different idea. But this was not an average friendship!

The dark day of separation came quickly. Scott and his family were moving! The boys horsed around. They kidded each other to keep from being too serious. They exchanged the rings. They said good by—and swallowed hard to keep from crying.

Chris was lonely and restless. He had other friends but Scott had been special. How he missed him! There was no one he could trust with his secrets. No one to do those extra special things with.

The days dragged by. Nothing seemed right. Chris wrote to Scott. Letters were hard to write. Not like seeing a friend. The ring helped, though. As time passed, it helped more and more.

How do you think the ring helped Chris? Do you think Chris's ring helped Scott, too? Write in your "Log for Journey of Faith" some ways it might have helped. Take time to do this. Don't read ahead until you have answered the question.

Do your answers suggest that the ring was like the Lord's Supper in any way? If so, how? Try to answer these questions. Put them in your log.

Here are some suggestions about how the ring and the Lord's Supper are alike. Can you think of others? Do you agree with these?

Ring	Lord's Supper
The ring was a symbol.	The Lord's Supper is a symbol.
The ring from Scott was a gift.	The Lord's Supper is a gift to us from Christ. It helps us in many ways.
The ring reminded Chris of his and Scott's friendship. They cared for each other.	The Lord's Supper reminds us of Christ's love for us and ours for him.
The ring stood for friendship.	The Lord's Supper stands for love.
The ring reminded Chris of Scott. When Chris looked at the ring Scott became real and present in Chris's memory. Scott was still a part of Chris's life.	The Lord's Supper makes Christ real to us. He truly is present as he shares the meal with us in Spirit. He is still a part of our lives.
The ring reminded Chris of what he and Scott had done together and what they had talked about.	The Lord's Supper reminds us of some of the things Jesus said and did, especially the greatest deed—his death on the cross.
The ring helped keep Chris's and Scott's friendship alive. It continued in their memory. It made them feel they were still together in spirit and mind.	The Lord's Supper helps us keep close to Jesus. It gives us strength to keep growing spiritually.

Celebrating the Lord's Supper with Meaning

How can we get the fullest meaning out of the celebration of the Lord's Supper? Most of us need help to do this. This sacrament can be a high moment of worship. Worship has to be learned. You can learn it. You can learn how to celebrate the Lord's Supper so it will do you good and also honor God. How can this be done? Try some of these suggestions.

1. *Think of Christ's inviting you to come.* To be invited puts you on the spot. You have to say yes or no. If it is just the matter of deciding whether you want to do it or not, it is easier. You answer only to yourself. If this is your attitude it is hard to find meaning in the sacrament. Christ does invite you. He said he wanted to eat the meal with the disciples. He arranged for a place and a time. He invited them to come. He invites you. He invites everyone. "Come to me, all of you who are tired . . . Take and eat it . . . Drink it, all of you." (Matthew 11:28; 26:26, *Good News Bible*). To believe these words puts your coming in a completely new light. You come in response to Christ's invitation.

2. *Come in faith.* The Lord's Supper is nothing in itself. It is just a series of acts and words. Merely going through the motions does nothing for God or us. It is faith that gives the meaning. So come in faith. Believe in Christ and trust him. Believe the bread to represent

his broken body. The wine to represent his blood shed for you. Faith makes the difference between mere emotions and true worship.

3. *Honor Christ.* Paul warned the Christians in Corinth against dishonoring Christ in the sacrament. (Read 1 Corinthians 11:27.) How can you honor Christ? By doing what he intended to have done in the sacrament. That is, celebrating God's love expressed through him. We are loved! God loves us. God shows this love to us through Christ. Remember Christ. Bring him to mind. Recognize his presence. Think of his life, his teaching, his death, his resurrection. Do this with joy and thanksgiving. Dedicate or rededicate yourself to him in joyful gratitude. This honors Christ.

4. *Center your attention on Christ.* You were told above to remember Christ. More needs to be added to this. Christ said, "Do this in remembrance of me." Keep Christ in the center of your thoughts. Think about him during the sacrament.

Christ always shared the nature of God. He gave this up to become a human being in obedience to God. In becoming one with us he suffered death. (Read Philippians 2:6-8.)

Remember Jesus Christ. You are not celebrating the death of an ordinary man. He lived a beautiful life in an ugly world. His goodness shamed the empty lives of the people about him. They killed him.

He loved the poor, the outcast, the sinful. He paid no heed to empty tradition. People got his attention. He loved them whether they loved him back or not. The way he lived and loved got him into trouble with those who ruled. He never changed. He was true to himself and God. He never let the threat of death stop him.

What a man! No wonder he saves us. He left an influence in the world. If we get close to him he will change us.

It is this man, this Son of God, whom we remember in the sacrament.

Jesus' love is reflected in the way a director of a Boys' Ranch loves the boys there. They come from broken homes, or just off the streets. They are not well trained. They often do criminal acts. The director told an audience that his car had been stolen by different boys twenty-six times! He usually found it. He brought each boy and the car back to the ranch. He did not punish them severely. He did lay some discipline on them. He did not get angry. He continued to love them and to keep working with them.

They were often surprised that he did not curse, beat, or imprison them. Sometimes they asked why. He told them he had met someone who had changed his life. Who was that? He told them of Jesus Christ.

Before going to your next communion read all you can about how Jesus loved. Read also the story of the crucifixion.

5. *Confess your sin.* In thinking about Jesus you may come to feel sinful. You see how far short of your best you fall. You know some things are wrong in your life. You may use bad words. You may be jealous of others. You may not care for other people. You may be unfair with some. You may not want to tell your feelings to anyone. You can tell them to God. God will forgive you. You can start all over again and improve. A feeling of relief and peace will come from the forgiveness you receive. One of the aims of the sacrament is to help you be free of sin, freed to follow Jesus. Confess your sins and enjoy forgiveness.

An eight-year-old girl felt alone and separated from her mother. She felt very guilty. Her mother had been trying to help her. Angry and bitter, the child ran out of the room and went upstairs. There she found a new dress that her mother was going to wear to a party that night. Nearby was a pair of scissors that her mother had been using. She picked up the scissors and cut the dress to pieces! She was getting even with her mother, hurting her.

In a little while the mother came up to the room. She saw what her daughter had done. She was heartbroken. She threw herself down on the bed and cried.

Pretty soon the little girl came in and walked slowly up to the bed. "Mother," she whispered. No reply. "Mother, mother, please," she begged again. After a moment the mother asked, "Please what?" "Please take me back, please take me back," prayed the little girl.

The mother reached out and took the daughter into her arms.

Have you ever done something to hurt someone else and been taken back in forgiveness? The mother taking her daughter back speaks of God's taking us back when we have acted badly. (*Man's Need and God's Action,* Reuel L. Howe, Seabury Press, pp. 132, 133).

6. *Share in the sacrament with others.* Holy communion is not a private sacrament. It is more than a matter between you and God alone. You share in it with others. Jesus said to the disciples, "All of you drink of it." He included everyone together.

Look around you at others in the service. You are one with them. You celebrate true communion by seeing that all of you belong together. "Red and yellow, black and white." You are all one family. You all belong to Christ. We all share in this family. We love, forgive, and work with each other. Think of this when you pass the bread and wine to your neighbor. You are saying you want to share with everyone!

Remember Key Meanings

Don't try to remember all these suggestions when you go to the Lord's Supper. Use the ones you seem to need most. Review the six statements above. Try to memorize them.

Some Things to Do

Before you close this book think of the meaning of the Lord's Supper. Recall a time you were in church when it was celebrated. Did you take part in it? Was it important to you? Would any of the suggestions made in this chapter have helped you? Which ones?

When will the Lord's Supper be celebrated again in your church? Write in your "Log for Journey of Faith" one or two meanings you will center your attention on. List two things you will do to help celebrate it properly.

Think of how the symbols of bread and wine fit the sacrament. They filled everyday needs. Bread was for hunger. Wine was for thirst. They were used daily in the Jewish homes of Palestine. Loaves were usually broken before being eaten. "Breaking bread" came to stand for a meal. The color of red wine suggests blood. Blood represents the life of a person. Can you think of some things Jesus said about wine, vines, wheat, bread?

Have you ever thought of the many movements and actions in the sacrament? We do a number of things. Jesus said, "This do. . . ." The sacrament is a thing to do, not merely to observe or say. The Lord's Supper is not the gospel in words. It is the gospel acted out. Just looking at the symbols is not enough. Meanings come from the actions. These include: being invited, coming, listening, breaking, pouring, taking, eating, drinking, tasting, sharing, confessing, thanking.

Jargon for the Journey

THE CUP: The cup of Bible times came in two general forms. One was like our cup and may or may not have had a handle. The other was a shallow bowl made in different forms and sizes. We have come to use the goblet or chalice as a symbol for the cup in the Lord's Supper.

ORTHODOX CHURCHES: Those churches came from the eastern section of the early church with headquarters in Constantinople. The eastern and western sections of the church separated in 1054.

ROMAN CATHOLIC CHURCH: The western section of the early church which became the church of which the Pope is head. Headquarters are in Rome. (*See Chapter 6.*)

CHAPTER XI
Living As a Christian

OUTWITTED

He drew a circle that shut me out—
Heretic, rebel, a thing to flout.
But Love and I had the wit to win:
We drew a circle that took him in!
—Edwin Markham

The symbol for living as a Christian is the circle of love which reaches out and takes in others.

Living As a Christian

Being a Christian is more than believing. It is more than being a member of the church. It is more than going to worship. It is more than learning about the Bible. It is being Christian, practicing Christianity in daily living. This chapter is written to help you learn what it means to live as a Christian.

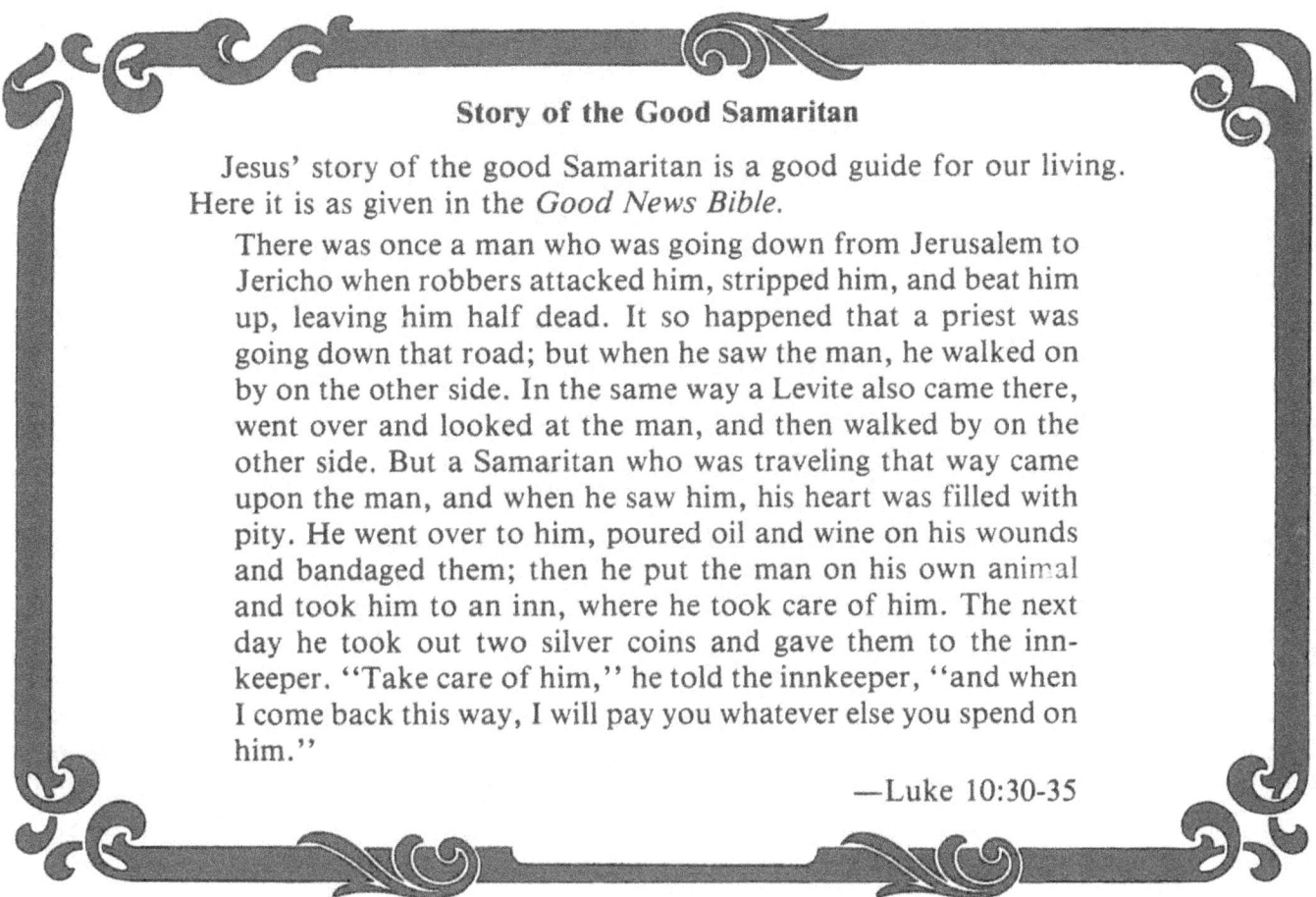

Story of the Good Samaritan

Jesus' story of the good Samaritan is a good guide for our living. Here it is as given in the *Good News Bible*.

> There was once a man who was going down from Jerusalem to Jericho when robbers attacked him, stripped him, and beat him up, leaving him half dead. It so happened that a priest was going down that road; but when he saw the man, he walked on by on the other side. In the same way a Levite also came there, went over and looked at the man, and then walked by on the other side. But a Samaritan who was traveling that way came upon the man, and when he saw him, his heart was filled with pity. He went over to him, poured oil and wine on his wounds and bandaged them; then he put the man on his own animal and took him to an inn, where he took care of him. The next day he took out two silver coins and gave them to the innkeeper. "Take care of him," he told the innkeeper, "and when I come back this way, I will pay you whatever else you spend on him."
>
> —Luke 10:30-35

Now read the same story told in another way. It is written from the viewpoint of the man who was attacked by the robbers.

Love in Action

A man is lying in the ditch beside the dusty road leading from Jerusalem to Jericho. He is a Jewish merchant. His head is covered with blood. One wound is oozing bloody water. The flies are buzzing around him. Ants are crawling over his body.

He groans. He opens one swollen eye and looks around. He is having a problem remembering. Where is he? What happened? His head is throbbing. His ears are ringing. Gradually he recalls a few things.

He had been heading for Jericho on a business trip. He had had a large sum of money in his money belt. The robbers, two bearded roughnecks, had attacked him with clubs. He had tried to fight them off but they had taken him by surprise. One of his arms is hurting. He had blocked a club with it. It is probably broken.

He suddenly thinks of his money. He lifts himself to his elbow, feeling the money belt. It is not there. All that money gone! "O God! I'm ruined. I had counted on that business deal to get ahead." Hopelessness overcomes him. He falls back to the ground. His wounds ache. His spirits sink low. He thinks of his family. And then he panics!

"I can't get out of this by myself out here on this lonely road and hurt bad." Is he going to die? He tries calling for help. All that comes out is a croak. A lone buzzard circles above.

Then he catches sight of a man on the road. Someone is coming toward him. His heart pounds. Help at last. A sense of relief floods through him. The man's dress is that of a priest. A priest who serves at regular times in the Jerusalem temple. A good man. A religious man. He will help.

But the priest hesitates. He stands at a distance. He thinks, "Poor man! The robbers got another victim. Something ought to be done about these criminals." He does not know whether the man is dead. He cannot touch a dead man. It would make him unclean according to the law. It would take days and days to be purified. He cannot run the risk. He has to lead worship in the temple. That is important, most important. The priest moves to the other side of the road and goes on his way, shaking his head.

The man in the ditch almost faints. It just cannot be happening. His hope fades. The flies buzz. The ants crawl. The gashes in his head ooze. His temples throb. The lone buzzard circles above. All is quiet. The hot sun beats down upon him.

Then he hears footsteps again! He opens his one good eye. It is a Levite, an officer and teacher in the temple. He has served a turn in the temple and is going to Jericho to rest. He sees the man in the ditch. He comes near. He stands by him and looks at him. His heart is touched. The man is really hurting. Tears come to the Levite's eyes. He says something.

He does nothing. The wounded man groans and tries to speak. Nothing comes out.

Then the Levite suddenly leaves and goes on down the road. He has plans of his own. He cannot afford to get involved. Besides, the robbers may still be near. He hurries along, almost running.

It is all over. Nobody is going to help. No chance for being saved. He is a goner. So he gradually goes out of his head and knows nothing more. . . .

He is aroused by someone touching him. His wounds are being examined. Healing oil and wine are being poured into them. He is now being lifted to the donkey the man had been riding. They are moving down the road.

How can this have happened? The man who stopped is a Samaritan! There are no good Samaritans. They are dogs. Jews and Samaritans have nothing to do with each other. They hate and distrust each other. One surely would not help the other. But it is happening. This Samaritan is taking him somewhere. He has tried to ease his pain. An amazing thing! A Samaritan stopping to help a Jew.

They begin to talk. He describes the attack in broken speech. The Samaritan says he is taking him to an inn down the road. He will spend the night with him. He will give the innkeeper money to care for him. The Samaritan will return and see what else can be done to help.

A feeling of gratitude fills the wounded man's mind and heart. And wonder and disbelief at what has happened. He cannot say enough to express his feelings. The Samaritan shrugs it off. It is only what any human being would do for another.

Love Leads to Action

This is a story of love in action. The Samaritan felt compassion for the wounded man. His heart was filled with pity. He wanted to help. He hurt with the Jew. But he did more than feel. He acted.

Love always acts. Love is always more than

feeling. More than words. "My children, our love should not be just words and talk; it must be true love, which shows itself in action." (1 John 3:18, *Good News Bible*)

> *Love led the Samaritan to do certain things.*
>
> 1. It led him to see a human being in need. He did not see a Jew. A Jew was an enemy of Samaritans. He did not see an enemy. He saw a man. Love does this for us. It opens our eyes to see human beings. Not the tags of names we give them—like whitey, nigger, mex, spic, wop, greaser.
>
> 2. It led him to go out of his way to help. He was on a journey, a business trip. He had an appointment. But he stopped, took time to get the man to the inn; spent the night with him; gave money to pay for his care. If we help others through love, we go out of our way. We give up some of the things we want to have and to do.
>
> 3. It led him to follow through on what he had started. He came back to look after the man. He did not start to help and then stop short. Helping others involves us. It takes time and trouble. It is not done quickly or easily.

Jesus told the story of the good Samaritan to teach us love: how to love and who to love; to do love, not merely to feel it; and to help anyone in any kind of need, anywhere. Jesus taught us not only in words or talk. He taught us by his life. He set an example for us.

We Learn Love from Jesus Christ

Jesus said, "As I have loved you, so you must love one another." (John 13:34, *Good News Bible*.) A Christian is one who loves as Jesus loved. A Christian is not only one who belongs to the church; attends worship; says kind words; believes the right things; feels with others. A Christian is one who loves; one who loves as Jesus loved.

And how did Jesus love?

Jesus loved selflessly. He helped others with no thought of getting anything in return.

He loved at a cost. He gave himself fully to others. He healed. His healing drained him of strength. He grew tired. He cared for others. He suffered inwardly with them. He felt what they felt. He died on the cross because he loved.

He loved with understanding. He knew from within what other people needed. He was aware of what they experienced. He tried to serve them in their need.

He loved everyone. He shut no one out. He loved others regardless of how they felt or acted toward him.

How did Jesus love?

See his love in action. See how he related to all kinds of people.

He loved children and they loved him. They liked to be around him. He liked to have them near him. "Some people brought their babies to Jesus for him to place his hands on them.

The disciples saw them and scolded them for doing so, but Jesus called the children to him and said, 'Let the children come to me and do not stop them. . . .' " (Luke 18:15-16, *Good News Bible*.)

He felt for the common people. He had compassion for them. When a multitude of five thousand came to hear him teach, he felt their hunger at meal time and fed them. (Read Matthew 14:13-21.) He saw what was in persons. He tried to help them to become their best. (Read John 1:42; Luke 19:1-10.)

He forgave sinners. He was kind to those who had done wrong. He did not condemn. He was not hard on them. He was kind to them. He felt for them. He kindled the spark of goodness in them. A modern-day disciple reports:

> "You could talk to Jesus about your problems and failures. He would not scold or put you down. He might not approve. But he would not treat you as if you were bad. He would look at you in the light of the good person you could become. You could trust him with your deepest secret about yourself. He would still accept and love you. Nothing could make him not love you."

The church leaders in Jesus' time became his enemies. They were afraid and jealous of him. They hated him. They plotted to kill him. He continued to teach them love. He tried to open God's love to them. (Read Luke 13:34, 35.)

He forgave his enemies. Even those who were crucifying him. He saw them as human beings who had lost their way. He never wanted to kill or hurt them. He wanted something better for them. (Read Luke 23:32-34.)

He was patient with his disciples. They were slow to learn. They found it hard to catch his spirit. He believed they could learn and grow. He was willing to trust his work to them when he died. He thought they would be true to him.

And how are we to love?

We are to love as Jesus loved.

I Know I Ought to Love Everybody, But . . .

Have you ever been in a situation which brought out more hate than love in you? Somebody hurting you? Saying unkind words? Pushing in front of you? Making fun of you?

Then you felt you ought to love rather than hate, but you wondered how you could. You may have said, "I know I ought to love everybody, but . . . " But what?

~~~~~~~~~~~~~~~~~~~~

But how can you love people who mistreat you?

But how can you love people who make you feel so little and unimportant?

But how can you love people whom you cannot trust? People who will take advantage of you?

But how can you love people who demand so much? They push everyone out of the way to get what they want.

But how can you love people who are so different from you?

But how can you love people you don't even like? And there are some you don't like at all!

~~~~~~~~~~~~~~~~~~~~

The truth about us is that we will not always

be able to love. We are human. We have weaknesses. We just will not be able to love every time. But we still know in our hearts that we ought to love. If we are serious about being Christian, we will want to learn how to love. We know we will have to keep working at it. One of the biggest lessons we have to learn is to love.

Who Will Help Us To Love When It Is So Difficult?

Love has to be kindled in our hearts, like starting a fire. You use little bits of paper and wood. You get the flame to start. Then you feed it larger and larger pieces of wood. You keep it going by putting wood on it from time to time. So with love, it has to be started, and it has to be fed.

How is this to be done? And who will do it? Jesus.

"We love because God first loved us." (1 John 4:19, *Good News Bible*.) God loved us through Jesus Christ. God loves us through other people, like father, mother, brother, sister, teacher, friend. This love given us kindles love in us. It helps us develop our ability to love. We love because we have first been loved. Jesus has loved us. He still loves us.

"The Spirit produces love." (Galatians 5:22, *Good News Bible*.) It is the Spirit of Christ in us that helps us to love. So we must keep open to the Spirit. The power to love does not come from us. We can try. We can make up our minds to love. We can put out all of our effort to love. But alone we cannot love. We love because the Spirit of Jesus Christ in us helps us. He loves through us.

We learn to love through practice. We will not always love as we should. We will have to ask forgiveness for failure. And keep practicing. We will need to keep open to Christ's Spirit so that he will be able to kindle love in us. And we will need to keep our eyes on Jesus who is our model and example in loving. As the years go by, we will learn more and more how to love.

The Symbol

Now look at the symbol for living as a Christian. Read the poem. In the symbol one person has drawn a circle and shut another out. There is an unhappy look on the first person's face. The second decides to draw a big circle with love and take the first one in. The second one is smiling. Joy comes when we are able to love.

What person or persons will you take in this week by drawing the circle of love around them?

Practice Sessions

Christian living and loving has to be learned. To learn it requires practice. This section contains suggestions for practicing love. Some of the drilling can be done by you alone. Some of it will have to be done with others. Take time to do as many of these exercises as you can.

An Exercise in Following the Golden Rule

Jesus tells us to treat others as we would like to be treated. (See Matthew 7:12.) This statement is often called "the Golden Rule." How would you like to be treated—
- —If you were a mother with a great deal of housework to do?
- —If you were your father or mother when demands for money are greater than the family income?
- —If you were a brother or sister who felt neglected and mistreated?

- If you were a person of one race in a community where the people of another race controlled everything?
- If you were an older person who has been in a nursing home for a year or longer?
- If you were a person of one race trying to be Christian in relation to the people of another race which is in the minority? in the majority?
- If you were in jail or a prison?
- If you were a girl or boy whose family could not afford to buy good clothes?
- If you were a new boy or girl in school?
- If you were a boy or girl who wanted to excel in sports but had been injured?
- If you were a girl or boy who seemed always to be making other people dislike you?
- If you were a member of a group who had been treated unjustly for generations?
- If you were a part of a minority/majority in school? community? nation?

(Adapted from material in *My Confirmation, A Guide for Confirmation Instruction,* United Church Press, 1963, page 93.)

A Practice in Making Choices

You meet situations every day in which you have to choose how to act and feel as a Christian. Use the following situations in practice sessions. Do these over a period of several days or weeks.

1. Think of a particular person who has hurt your feelings. You are angry. You feel hateful things toward that person. You want to get even. As a Christian, how are you going to handle the feelings? How are you going to act toward that person?

2. Think of a person who always pushes ahead of you and others for privileges, place, honor, recognition, and so on. How would you feel toward that person? Should you try to stop her/him? Talk to her/him? Talk to your teacher? Push her/him out of the way? Fight her/him? Or . . .

3. You are in a group who are telling dirty or racial jokes. Each person seems to be trying to outdo the others. As a Christian, what will you do? Tell a joke? Walk away? Lecture the group? Be silent? Or . . .

4. You are in a group who are gossiping about another person. You know the person. Some things being said are untrue. Some are true so far as you know. As a Christian, what will you do? Walk away? Defend the person? Try to get them to stop? Ask them what all of you can do to help the person? Or . . .

5. Some kids you know may smoke tobacco, use drugs, speak profanity, drink alcohol, talk about boys and girls in suggestive ways, steal and lie. As a Christian, what will be your attitude toward the persons who do these things? Is participation in any of these activities to be a part of the Christian life?

6. You know people who are sick, in nursing homes, shut-in, lonely and neglected? As a Christian, do you feel responsible for doing something for them? Why?

7. You know some new families who have moved into the community. As a Christian, is there something you should do for them? What?

8. You know of some poor people in the community. They are having a hard time getting enough food and clothing. As a Christian, what can you or your church do to help? Will you help?

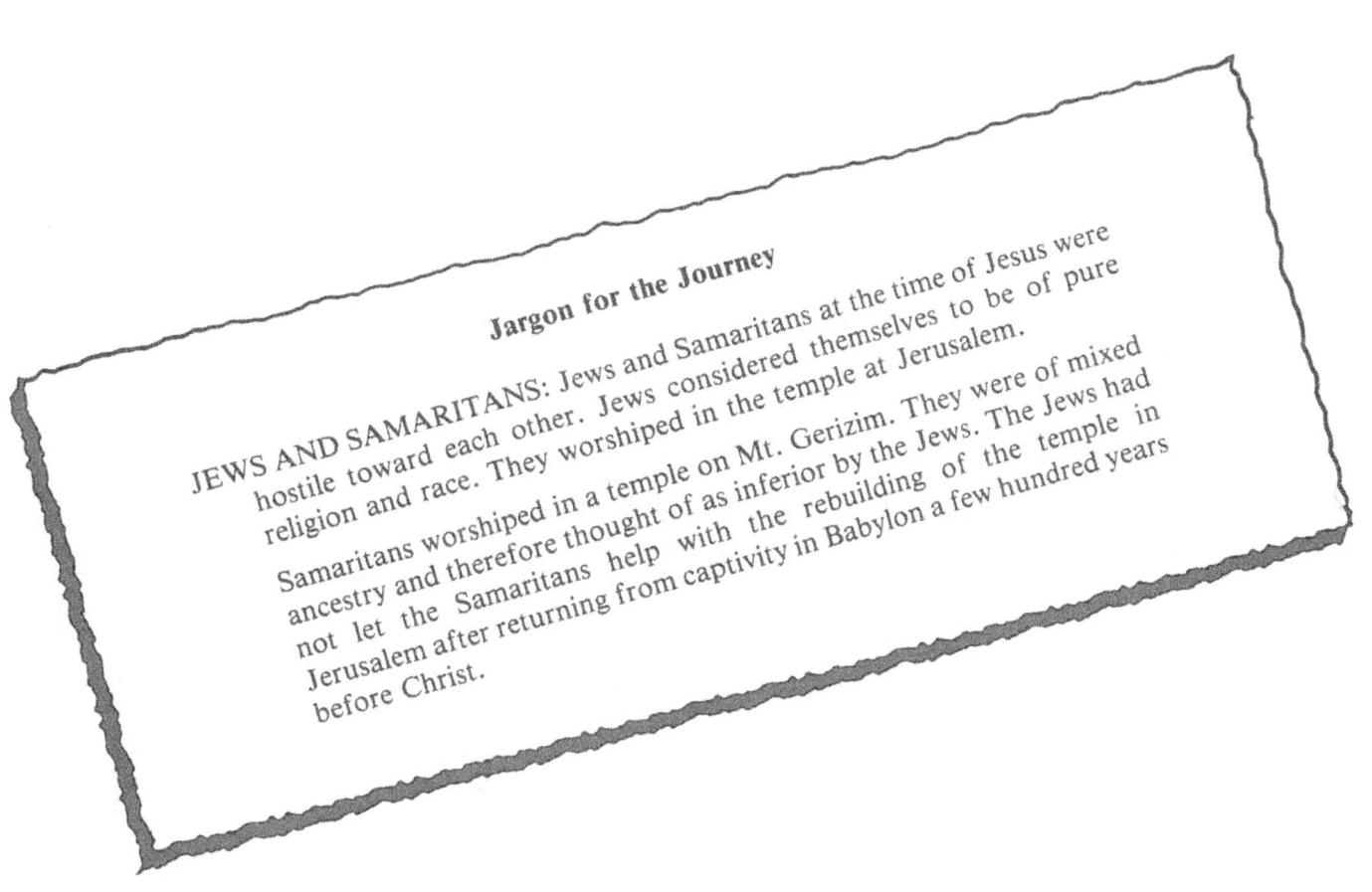

Jargon for the Journey

JEWS AND SAMARITANS: Jews and Samaritans at the time of Jesus were hostile toward each other. Jews considered themselves to be of pure religion and race. They worshiped in the temple at Jerusalem. Samaritans worshiped in a temple on Mt. Gerizim. They were of mixed ancestry and therefore thought of as inferior by the Jews. The Jews had not let the Samaritans help with the rebuilding of the temple in Jerusalem after returning from captivity in Babylon a few hundred years before Christ.

CHAPTER XII

Our Commitment

The cross is the symbol for our commitment to Christ and his Church, for in our commitment we answer his call to come, take up our cross.

Our Commitment

*"Take my life and let it be
Consecrated, Lord, to Thee."*

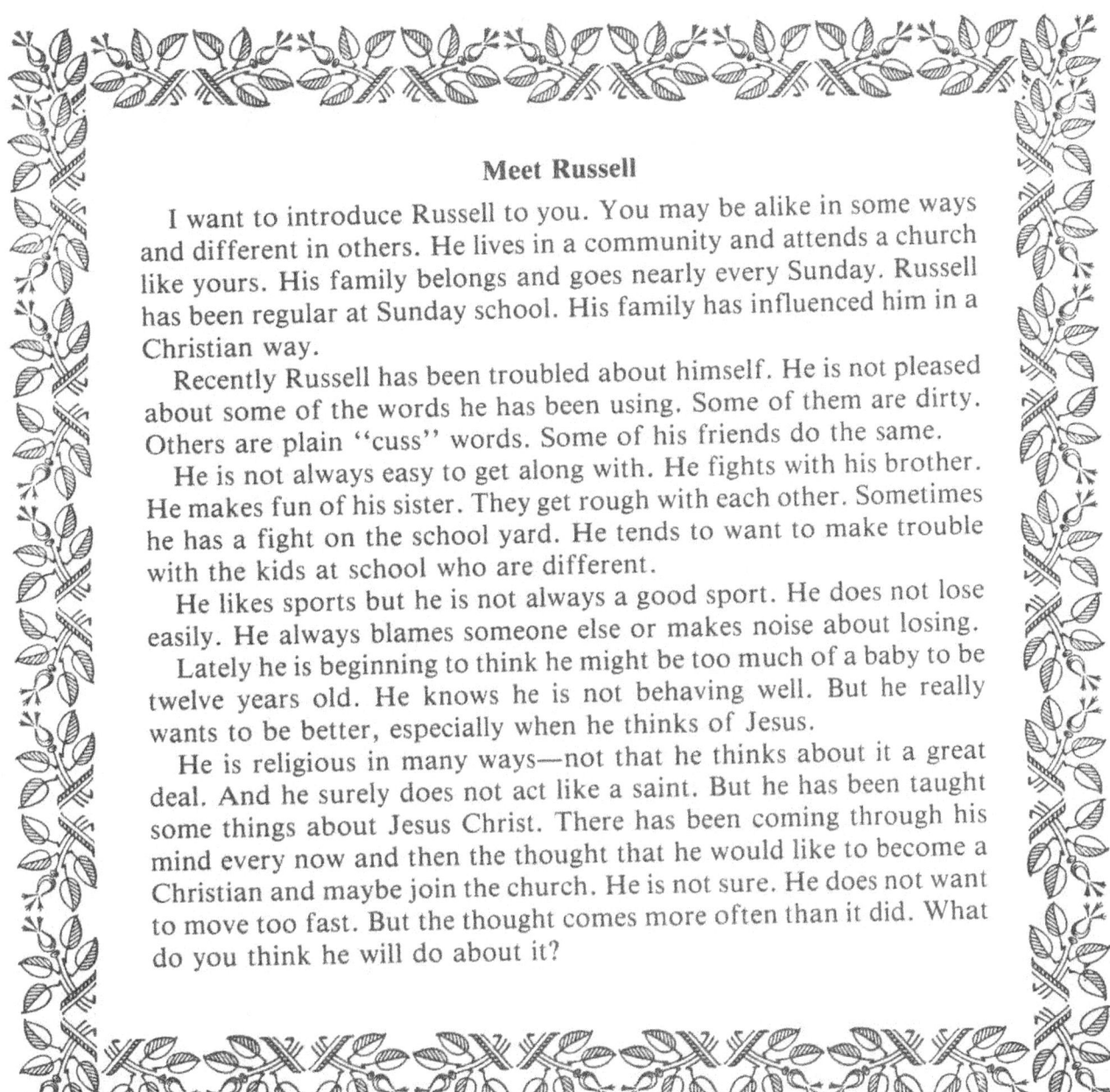

Meet Russell

I want to introduce Russell to you. You may be alike in some ways and different in others. He lives in a community and attends a church like yours. His family belongs and goes nearly every Sunday. Russell has been regular at Sunday school. His family has influenced him in a Christian way.

Recently Russell has been troubled about himself. He is not pleased about some of the words he has been using. Some of them are dirty. Others are plain "cuss" words. Some of his friends do the same.

He is not always easy to get along with. He fights with his brother. He makes fun of his sister. They get rough with each other. Sometimes he has a fight on the school yard. He tends to want to make trouble with the kids at school who are different.

He likes sports but he is not always a good sport. He does not lose easily. He always blames someone else or makes noise about losing.

Lately he is beginning to think he might be too much of a baby to be twelve years old. He knows he is not behaving well. But he really wants to be better, especially when he thinks of Jesus.

He is religious in many ways—not that he thinks about it a great deal. And he surely does not act like a saint. But he has been taught some things about Jesus Christ. There has been coming through his mind every now and then the thought that he would like to become a Christian and maybe join the church. He is not sure. He does not want to move too fast. But the thought comes more often than it did. What do you think he will do about it?

Profession and Commitment

Have you, like Russell, considered making a profession of faith and becoming a committed church member? Do you have problems you are concerned about? How ready do you think you are for this step? Have you been feeling lately that you may decide to do it? This chapter will help you understand better what it means to make a commitment to Christ and the church.

To make a profession is to declare your faith

in Jesus Christ publicly. To become a committed church member is to decide on your own to give yourself to Christ and the church. You will answer the questions in the church covenant with "I do" or "I will" or in some other fitting way. This voluntary act is a response to God's call.

According to the New Testament there is no such person as a Christian apart from the church. The Christian cannot stand alone, separated from fellow Christians and Christ. You, as a Christian, draw strength from Christ and the church. You serve in and through the church. You represent Christ and the church wherever you go. The Christian, Christ, and the church are bound together by promises made to each other.

Profession and commitment are to be made of your own free choice. Your reason for taking the step should not come from a feeling that it is the thing to do; or that you are old enough; or that your parents, pastor, or other adults want you to take the step; or that other young people your age are doing it. Nor should your reason be that you have enrolled in a class on church membership.

Your profession and commitment are to be your own free response to an inner call of the Spirit. When Jesus was on earth he called people to believe in and to follow him. This call continues to come to us today. It comes sooner or later to every person. You do not hear a human voice calling your name. You experience it in your heart. You sense an urgency inside to come to Christ and to give yourself to the church.

Boys and girls your age are not too young to know this call. You make up your own mind whether to respond or not. The call comes before any desire or intention on your part to come to Christ. When you first feel this "drawing" of the Spirit, you know God is inviting you to become God's child. Jesus said, "No one can come to me unless the Father who sent me draws him to me." (John 6:44, *Good News Bible*.)

Unless you have felt this call, do not commit yourself. If the call is real, consider an answer. But you do not have to respond at the moment. God gives us freedom. God does not rush anyone. You have to decide for yourself when you are ready. This does not mean you ought to put it off for a long time. It does mean that you have a free choice and time to think it over.

Up to this point in your journey of faith you have probably accepted the faith of your family and church. You may now decide by choice whether you are going to make it your own. Others have probably taught you that God loves and calls you. You may have believed it and agreed to it in your own mind.

Now you feel God's call. Or, you may have been feeling the call for some time. Now you are faced with having to make a personal decision. No decision is quite so important.

Your profession and commitment are not a promise to be perfect. You will never be perfect on earth. You are turning your back on what is wrong. You are asking forgiveness for past failures. You are taking one more forward step in your journey of faith. You are getting in deeper. You are wanting to be Christian in more and more ways. Your goal is to become more Christian, more like Christ "until Christ's nature is formed in you." (Galatians 4:19, *Good News Bible*.)

Your emotions are involved in the act of commitment. Some people are deeply stirred in the experience. Others are more calm and quiet. Either way is all right. Not everyone feels the same. Let yours be natural for you. Try not either to force or to hold back your emotions. Let them flow as they come.

The words used often to describe the experience of call and response are: Awakening, Conversion, and New Birth. These three words describe the same experience in a little different way.

Awakening refers to being made to feel alive to God: to become aware of God's presence; to be made more conscious of the working of the Spirit in your life; to become more concerned about your relation to God.

Conversion means being changed in your purposes and actions. Christ changes you into a productive and useful person. "The Spirit produces love, joy, peace, patience, kindness, goodness, faithfulness, humility, and self-control." (Galatians 5:22, 23, *Good News Bible*.)

New Birth means being created anew, to be born again spiritually. You are born of the Spirit. It is like beginning all over again with new spiritual life in you. "When anyone is joined to Christ, he is a new being; the old is gone, the new has come." (2 Corinthians 5:17, *Good News Bible*.)

The Church Covenant

If you decide to become a committed church member, the pastor will ask you the questions in the church covenant. The covenant will be given in a public service of worship. He or she will discuss these questions with you beforehand. You can ask your pastor what they will be.

In giving your answers you will be stating things you believe and intend to do. They will include something like the following five statements. These define what it means for you to be a committed church member. Your commitment will be lived out in your world—which is largely home, church, and school. Later on, as you grow, you can take other steps forward.

When you become a committed church member you are saying:

1. I repent of my sin. I believe and accept Jesus Christ to be my Savior and the Lord of my life.
What is sin and who is a sinner? Sin can be defined in many ways. For one, it means missing the mark. A grandfather and a grandson went out with an air rifle for target practice. They set up a target with a bull's-eye surrounded by circles. They tried to hit the center mark, the bull's-eye. They came close a number of times. But they kept missing the mark. Sometimes they hit within the circles. A few times they missed the whole thing.

We have within us great possible good. We are made in the image of God, that is, in God's nature. We can relate to God, know God, love God, love people, help others, think good thoughts, be unselfish and useful. We can do much good in the world. To sin is to miss the mark, to fail to be and do what we can. All of us sin. We never reach the highest level of which we are capable. "Everyone has sinned, everyone has fallen short of the beauty of God's plan." (Romans 3:23, *Phillips*.)

Are you a sinner as described above? Have you ever: hated someone? been uninterested when someone was hurt? refused to care when people have no food? been jealous of someone? envious because someone had something you did not have? fought and fussed with brother or sister? used dirty words? been selfish? If so, you have missed the mark.

God forgives you when you confess that you have missed the mark. God continues to call you to a truer life. You can improve. God never gives up on you. God never ceases to call you to a better life and to believe in you.

"I repent of my sin." To repent means to be sorry for failing. To turn away from it. To resolve to live more like a Christian with Christ's help. "I have the strength to face all conditions by the power that Christ gives me" (Philippians 4:13, *Good News Bible*.)

"I believe." You confess and accept Jesus Christ as your Savior. You are saying publicly that you believe in Jesus Christ as God's Son who forgives your sin, accepts you and brings you close to God.

You confess that Jesus Christ is Lord. You become his follower. You take the lead from him in daily living. As Lord he has the final word about your life. You say you want to obey him and to live as he teaches you to live. You want him and his Spirit to rule your life. "For us . . . there is only one Lord, Jesus Christ, through whom all things were created and through whom we live." (1 Corinthians 8:6, *Good News Bible*.)

2. I believe the Bible to be the inspired Word of God, the true guide for faith and practice. I will read and study it for guidance in living the Christian life.

You have already studied the chapter on the Bible. Turn back to it and look it over briefly. This will renew your memory of its main teachings.

When you become a committed member of the church you are promising to read and study the Bible. It is not enough to say you believe it to be God's Word. You must use it. It will guide you always in your faith and life as a Christian. There will never come a time when you do not need it. A road map helps you reach your goal on an automobile trip. The Bible guides you on your journey of faith.

You are expected to study the Bible in Sunday school, small groups, and privately. You will also be helped by hearing the minister preach the Word.

Reading the Bible alone and with others can also be a help and a joy. Have you begun using the list of readings at the end of the chapter on the Bible?

3. I promise to be a faithful member of the church.

Faithful means loyal. You promise to be true to the church's nature and purpose. You will support it. You will do all you can to make it better. Here are at least three things you can do in being faithful:

a. *Attend worship regularly.* How often does that mean? At least once every Sunday. Boys and girls, and sometimes adults, do not want to go every Sunday. They offer excuses. However, worship is important. It is necessary to your life as a Christian. You gain strength from gathering together. By worshiping you keep God in the center of your life. The very life of the church depends on its worship. Worship for the Christian is like food and water to the body.

Interview at least five persons: a boy or girl your age; a teenager; someone in their twenties; a middle-aged person; and an older person. Ask them: Why do you go to worship? Do you think it is important? Why? How does it help you in your Christian life? Record the answers in your "Log for Journey of Faith." Share the answers in your next class meeting.

b. *Serve in and through the church.* The church has been given a big job. It is to share the gospel with everyone everywhere. Teach Christ. Serve people in any need. Work for friendship in the world.

"Go, then, to all peoples everywhere and make them my disciples: baptize them in the name of the Father, the Son, and the Holy Spirit, and teach them to obey everything I have commanded you. And I will be with you always, to the end of the age." (Matthew 28:19-20, *Good News Bible*.)

"God . . . through Christ changed us from enemies into his friends and gave us the task of making others his friends also. Our message is that God was making all mankind his friends through Christ." (2 Corinthians 5:18-19, *Good News Bible*.)

What can you and other boys and girls do to serve in the church? Ask your pastor. Talk it over with your Sunday school teacher. Your father or mother may have some ideas. Write these in the "Log." Plan to serve in some way.

Could you do something like this: Visit the people in a nursing home? Take some food to a poor family? Read to a person who is blind or cannot read? Visit a person who is shut-in? Baby-sit for free for a young couple who need help?

c. *Be loving and caring toward the church members.* A popular song in recent years said "What the world needs now is love, sweet love." 1 Corinthians 13:13, *Good News Bible*, says "These three remain: faith, hope, and love; and the greatest of these is love." One of the best things you can do is to spread love in the church. Share your life in loving and caring with all members, but particularly with those who have special needs. You are young but you can learn to love more and more.

Love is more than a good feeling toward others. Love is wanting good for others and trying to see that they get it. To do this you will have to give time and energy and yourself. You will have to give up some things you want for others to have what they want and need. It costs us something to love. The cross was the cost for Christ. In spite of this, what the world needs most is "love, sweet love."

Marilyn, a young white woman, was a victim of infantile paralysis—polio. She spent hours a day in an iron lung. Her arms and legs were so weak and thin she could not walk. Her mother took her downtown every afternoon. She would sit in the car and watch the people.

She began to notice a little black girl watching her at times. Her name was Melissa. She had heard of Marilyn and her illness. She felt sorry for her. She wanted to help but she was timid. She would look at her from a distance, then run off.

Finally Melissa got up nerve enough to come closer and closer. She ran up to Marilyn one day and dropped a dime in her lap and ran away fast. This was her way of saying "I care."

Marilyn was really touched by what Melissa did. She wanted to know who she was. She finally found out and asked Melissa to come and sit with her a few hours a day. Arrangements were made to pay Melissa for her services. She helped Marilyn for a number of years. They became close friends.

Marilyn was a member of the Cumberland Presbyterian Church. Melissa was a Methodist. They knew how to love. (This story is true.)

Write one thing in the "Log for Journey of Faith" you will do this week to show love to someone in the church.

4. I will try hard to overcome temptation and weakness and to grow as a Christian. You know what temptation is. You have experienced it. You, like all of us, are tempted to do wrong, to take it easy, just to get by, to fall below the best. Because you are a human being you will fail sometimes and regret it. But you will also win at times.

You are in a contest. Life is a battle between good and evil. You have to keep fighting. God will help you. But God cannot fight your battles for you. You have to do that. Strength is developed by struggle. Muscles grow through tension. So does character and Christian faith and life.

It is not easy to live the Christian life. However, nothing gives more challenge. There is no joy like that of overcoming. Through God's help you win the battle. So keep up the fight. Don't throw in the towel.

You overcome temptation by trying. It is doubtful if you grow by trying. You grow by getting the right food for your body, mind, and spirit. So feed on Christ. Learn more about him. Study your Bible. Worship. Pray. Draw help from the church.

You grow by what God gives you. Keep open to God. God gives you grace. Grace is "influence from God acting in you to help you live a good life." Let that influence come into your life every day. Jude, verse 21 says, "Keep yourselves in the love of God." (*Good News Bible*.) A house plant grows by staying in the sunlight. Our spirits grow by staying in God's love and grace. God often influences us through other people.

You grow by exercise. You learn by practicing. This is how you learn to play a musical instrument, or football, basketball, soccer, or baseball. This is how you learn to worship and love. This is how you learn to serve, to forgive, to understand. Practice. Do it over and over. You can and will learn and grow.

What one thing will you do this week to learn and grow? Write it in your "Log."

5. I will be a good steward.

A steward looks after that which belongs to someone else. We are stewards. God has trusted us to care for, develop and use life, talents, time, and money. They are not ours. They are gifts of trusts. We have to answer to God for them.

How well are you doing with them? Right now as a young person you hardly know your talents. Your job ahead is to find what they are and develop them for good use. What do you think may be some of your abilities? Ask some other people what they think your talents may be. List them in the "Log."

How do you use your time? Do you keep a good balance of time for playing, studying, helping in the home, worshiping, reading, eating, sleeping, listening to music, watching TV, being with family and friends? Make a chart of how you use an average day, showing the time spent in each activity. Record your chart in the "Log."

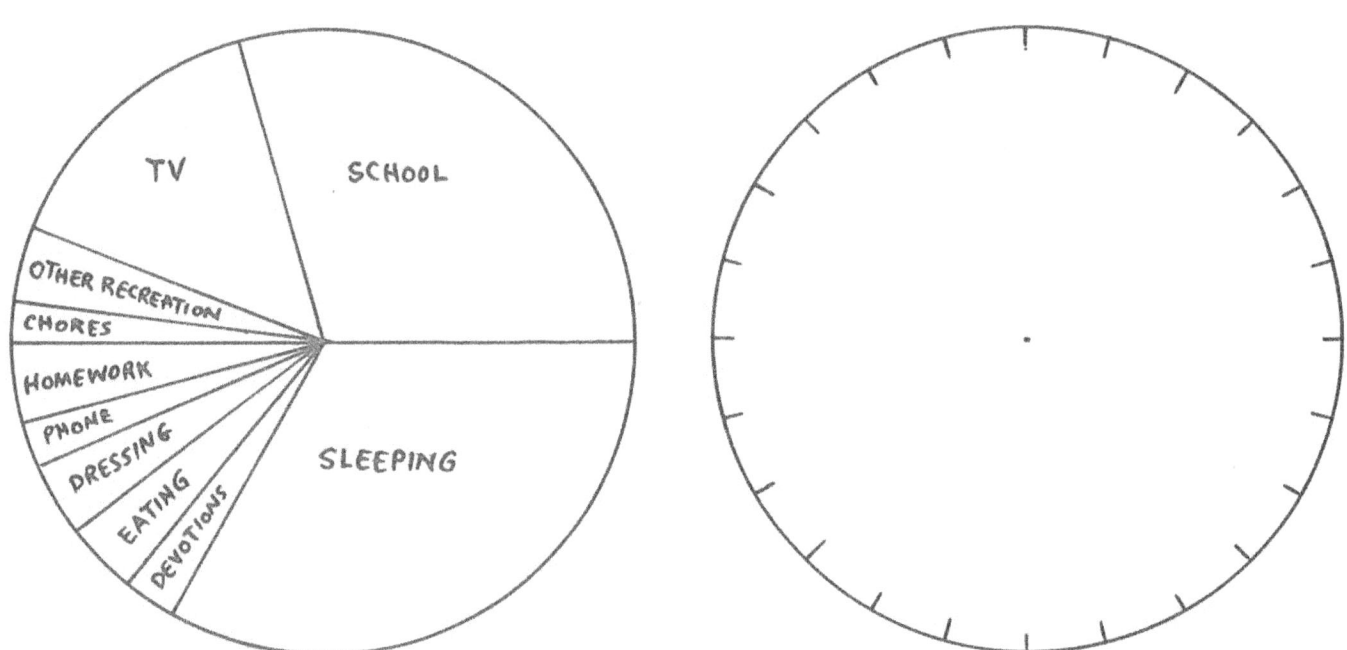

How well do you use your money? Where do you get it? How do you spend it? You probably depend on an allowance from your family. You may work some and make a little for yourself.

You are trusted with money. Being a good steward has to do with how you get it and how you spend it. What is the best guide for giving your money to the church?

Some Christians practice tithing. A tithe is a tenth of one's income. The people of the Old Testament gave a tenth because it was required. It was in obedience to the law. They made other offerings in addition to the tithe. They felt the tithe was holy. It was a duty for them to give it. Not to give it was to rob God.

Christians who tithe today are not under the law. They are under the new covenant of grace and love. They give because they love Christ and want to give. They give out of gratitude for all God has done for them. They feel that the least they can do is to give a tenth out of love. "Each one should give, then, as he has decided, not with regret or out of a sense of duty; for God loves the one who gives gladly." (2 Corinthians 9:7, *Good News Bible*.)

The Christian is not limited in giving. We are not bound to give a certain amount. People who have less money are free to give less. People who have more money are free to give more.

What is your reaction to these thoughts about giving? Will you consider following them as a guide? Discuss this with your pastor and parents.

Review

Turn back to the first of the five statements about the church covenant. Read the statements aloud.

This chapter has covered many important ideas regarding your becoming a committed church member. If you have problems with some of these ideas, discuss them with a parent or your pastor.

The church covenant may seem to demand a great deal of you. Is it asking too much? What would you leave out? Becoming a committed church member is the greatest step in your life. You need to take it seriously or not at all. Shining through all the demands is the light of God's grace at every step. Joining in the struggle for spiritual growth and achievement will bring you joy. "Let us keep our eyes fixed on Jesus, on whom our faith depends from beginning to end. He did not give up because of the cross! On the contrary, because of the joy that was waiting for him, he thought nothing of the disgrace of dying on the cross. . . ." (Hebrews 12:2, *Good News Bible*.)

When you decide to make your profession and commit yourself to the church, write the five statements above in the "Log" and sign them. You will discuss this step with your parents and pastor before taking it.

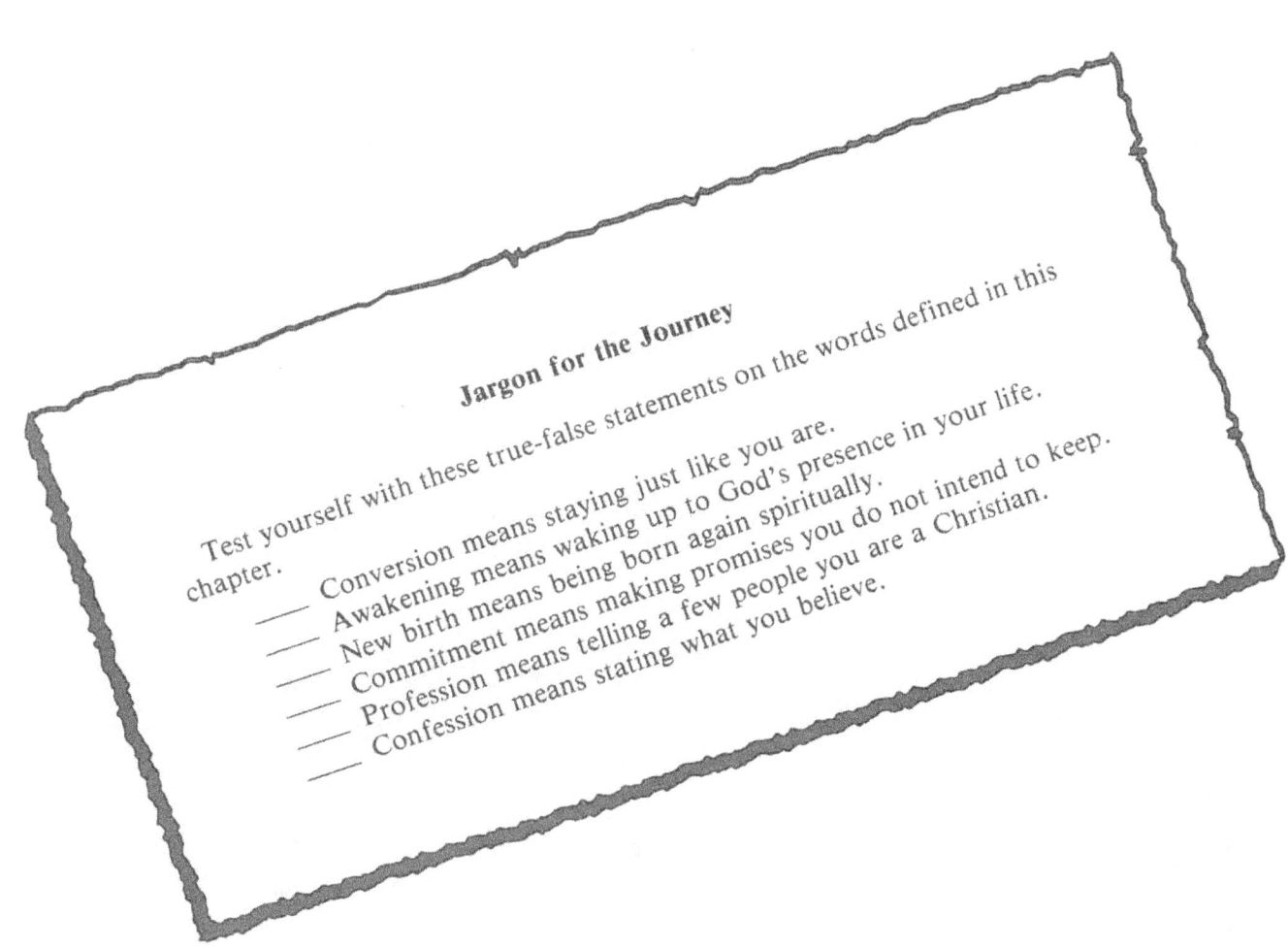

Jargon for the Journey

Test yourself with these true-false statements on the words defined in this chapter.

___ Conversion means staying just like you are.
___ Awakening means waking up to God's presence in your life.
___ New birth means being born again spiritually.
___ Commitment means making promises you do not intend to keep.
___ Profession means telling a few people you are a Christian.
___ Confession means stating what you believe.

CHAPTER XIII
Christian Growth

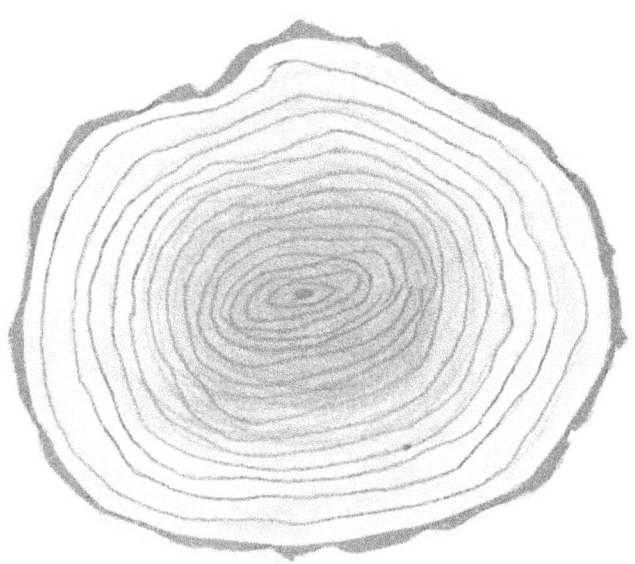

This is a cross section of a tree. The outer ring is the growing edge, just under the bark. The new wood is white and soft. The older the tree is, the harder and more colorful the wood becomes. See the dark center in the cross section above.

Count the growth rings of a tree to determine its age. Some rings are wider than others. The tree grows more in the years of greater rainfall. We grow faster when we have more of the water of life, Jesus Christ.

Every living thing has a growing edge. In this chapter we look to the growing edge of our lives.

Christian Growth

"We are to grow up in every way . . . into Christ." (Ephesians 4:15, *Revised Standard Version*.)

Your journey of faith never ends. The true Christian experience is one of continual growth. The Bible teaches the need for the new birth in Jesus Christ. It also says much about Christian growth.

Birth is only the beginning. Growth is normal. It is expected in all living things. It is the way toward completeness. People expect us to grow. They think we will grow at a certain rate. There are ways we are expected to act at certain stages of growth. Growth in body, mind, spirit, attitude, and behavior is hoped for.

This chapter has to do with our growth as Christians.

Grow Up, Charlie Brown!

Linus, Lucy, and Charlie Brown are talking about growing up. Woodstock and Snoopy are listening in.

Linus: I marked my height again this morning on the wall in my room. I've grown a half inch in the last six months. Gosh, I'm so small! I don't know if I will ever be over five feet.

Charlie Brown: I checked myself too not long ago. I'm a half inch shorter than I was this time last year. Sigh!!!! I grow in reverse.

Lucy: I'm tall enough. Who wants to grow? That's silly. People who want to grow are insecure.

Snoopy (aside): When you are one of a litter of eight pups, survival and not growth is what you think about.

Woodstock: ′′′′′′ ′′ ′′ ′′′′′′ ′′′′′′′′′ (Which being translated means: All I want is to be big enough so people can see me.)

Linus: The Bible says we are to grow "in grace and knowledge." (2 Peter 3:18.) That's the kind of growth that really matters.

Lucy: There you go again, Linus, trying to show off. Why are you always quoting the Bible like a preacher? You don't impress me. (To herself: I wonder what grace means.)

Charlie Brown: Linus, what does it mean to grow in grace?

Linus: It means getting to the place you can lose without going bananas.

Charlie Brown: That'll be the day! I thought it meant to be able to win just once!

Snoopy: Dogs are more interested in bones than grace.

Woodstock: I thought grace was being able to get to the worm first.

Linus has thrown us a curve. He has used a phrase we may not know. What does it mean to grow in grace? One dictionary says: "Grace is the influence of God in our lives to make us spiritually strong. It makes us able to be and do what we could not do on our own." Do you understand what this means? To grow in grace means to be able to be more Christian in more situations. Here are some examples of this:

Growing in the Ability to Handle Conflict

Mark was at bat in the softball game between the Cumberland Presbyterian and Methodist teams. He hit the ball hard. It should be a double, he thought. Running fast, he slid into second. Joe Harkness, a kid he knew in the sixth grade, tagged him hard. It felt like he had broken a rib. Mark jumped up saying some pretty bad words to Joe. He hit Joe with his fist. One of the umpires stopped them or they would have had a big fight. When the boys cooled down, the game continued.

After he had gotten under control, Mark thought about what he had said and done. He had mixed feelings about it. Joe had no

business tagging him so hard. But that did not excuse him for losing his temper. He said nothing to anyone about how he felt.

Days passed. He thought about apologizing to Joe. But then, why didn't Joe apologize to him? He talked to his older sister Pat about it. Pat would not tell him what to do. She just let him talk it out.

After a few days Mark decided to go to Joe and straighten things out. He apologized. He and Joe continued to be friends. Mark felt much better about himself.

What had helped him do this? Grace and growth. In working out his behavior in this matter he had grown some. He acted a little more like a grown up and a little less like a child. The reason he could do it was because he received some help from God. God gave him grace.

Learning to Be Kind and Understanding

Jason lived long ago when the church was very young. He grew in his ability to care for others. He went to synagogue school with

youth his age. Rabbi David taught them. They sat on the floor together. They read often from the scrolls containing the Scriptures. Some could read well. Others could not.

Caleb was from a poor family. His parents were not well educated. Caleb had a hard time. He could not read well. He stuttered. He was nervous and always seemed uneasy.

Rabbi David thought he could help Caleb by making him read. So he called on him often.

But the more he had to read the more he stuttered. The other students laughed at him. After class he would go off by himself. Sometimes he cried.

One day after Caleb had a very bad time, Jason went to him. He began to talk with Caleb. He showed him he cared. Caleb began to relax. He stopped crying. He knew he had a friend who understood.

Jason began to go to Caleb often after class. When Jason was around, Caleb seemed to relax and to stutter less. This helped to improve Caleb's reading. Each time he was called upon, he knew Jason cared.

We, too, can learn to be kind and understanding. That is much better than laughing at others who have problems.

Learning to Take Criticism

Lucy was freckle-faced. She had a runny nose. She was always sniffling. But Lucy was outspoken. She had an opinion on everything. She studied her lessons. She took part in class. Sometimes she showed that she was much brighter than others.

This behavior made others be unkind to Lucy. They criticized her. They did their best

to find fault with her. They would make fun of her and her ideas. Their criticism hurt Lucy. But she kept right on doing what she did.

One day a report was due in class. It was to be on space travel. The students were to imagine what the future would be like; when space travel would increase; what kind of planes would be used; whether life on other planets would be discovered. There were some imaginative ideas expressed, but none so fantastic as Lucy's. And the others made fun of her.

This was the worst time she had had. They really got through to her. She felt like she did not have a friend in the whole class. She felt all alone. That night in bed she cried and then cried because she had cried. She thought she was being a baby to cry. And she had hard feelings toward those who had laughed at her.

Then, Lucy decided that she might be to blame for some of this trouble. She might be talking too much; trying too hard to be different; trying to show up the others. So she worked at taming herself down a bit.

After several weeks of this, things did not seem to change very much. Others still criticized and made fun of Lucy. It still hurt. But gradually she began to take criticism a little better. She began to see herself more and more as others saw her. And she saw that she was causing some of their behavior.

One day in class when Lucy was spouting off some of her opinions, everyone laughed. And she laughed, too, at herself. This took the sting off a little. And she felt she was growing some. She had quit trying to show up the others. She was not quite so outspoken. And she could look at herself and see what she had been doing. A part of her change came about because she had been asking God to help her.

Have you ever had a problem anything like this? What are you doing to improve and grow?

Outgrowing Jealousy

Jenny is jealous of her older brother Adam. She really does not like him. He is always hard on her. He seems to resent her being around. He plays pranks on her. He gets into her stuff and messes up her room.

Being older, Adam seems to get all the privileges. He gets to go places she doesn't go and do things she doesn't do. Being a boy he seems to have more freedom than she has. She has become angry and resentful. So she cries, fusses, complains, yells, and often tries to pay him back for what he does to her.

None of this has any effect on him. He keeps right on making her miserable. And he

does not care at all. One thing is sure. He is not going to change yet. Any change depends on her. What can she do?

Jenny may not be able to solve this problem right now. But there is a force at work in us to move us toward completion. It is the way God made us. God works in us to help us grow up. God is working in Jenny in this way.

There was a little boy who sucked his thumb. His father and mother did all they could to break him of it. They put red pepper on it. They scolded him. They shamed him. They tied it so he could not get it into his mouth. He kept on sucking his thumb. One day he stopped. They noticed it. They said something to him about it. He replied, "Big boys don't suck their thumbs."

Some day Jenny may get to the place where she can say, "Big girls are not jealous of their brothers." Or, "Christians grow out of their resentments."

God is at work in Adam, too. Some day he may grow up.

You Can Grow

The examples we have used tell how some people change and grow. You, too, can become the kind of person you want to be. You can change and grow into the kind of person God intends for you to become. He calls us and sets us apart to be like Christ. He works within us and gives us growth.

"We know that in all things God works for good with those who love him, those whom he has called according to his purpose. Those whom God had already chosen he also set apart to become like his Son. . . ." (Romans 8:28-29, *Good News Bible*.)

How Can You Grow

It takes time. You do not grow up quickly because you wish it. You will not wake up tomorrow as a full-grown person because you ask God for a miracle or because you will and want this deeply for yourself. Life unfolds gradually from within. Your body grows gradually for a number of years. So does your mind. It takes time for the Spirit to produce "love, joy, peace, patience, kindness, goodness, faithfulness, humility, and self control." (Galatians 5:22-23, *Good News Bible*.)

So give yourself time to grow up. Read Jesus' parable of the growing seed in Mark 4:26-29.

Keep in touch with Christ. Do this through worship, prayer, meditation, the sacraments, sermons, and reading the Bible. Do this also through Christian fellowship, Sunday school, camps, and conferences. "Since you have accepted Christ Jesus as Lord, live in union with him. Keep your roots in him, build your lives on him, and become stronger in your faith, as you were taught." (Colossians 2:6-7, *Good News Bible*.)

A beautiful symbol of our relationship with Christ is given in John 15:1-5. Jesus uses the figure of the vine and branches to teach us to keep in touch with him in order to grow. Read this passage.

We grow by effort, struggle, and pain. Growth is not easy. It comes hard. It often includes pain and struggle. It is difficult to change and grow. Have you ever had the "leg ache?" Sometimes this happens when we are young. Such aches are sometimes referred to as "growing pains." We can experience these pains in other types of growth, too.

For instance, it is hard to grow enough to forgive some people. We have to struggle to learn the lesson of unselfishness. If often hurts to learn patience, to wait for some things to happen, like getting certain privileges.

Examples in nature tell us the same thing. For the chicken to become free, it has to break through its shell. For the snake to continue to grow, it has to get out of its outgrown skin. Before the caterpillar can become a butterfly, it has to die as a worm. These experiences are painful.

"For this very reason do your best to add goodness to your faith; to your goodness add knowledge; to your knowledge add self-control; to your self-control add endurance; to your endurance add godliness; to your godliness add brotherly affection; and to your brotherly affection add love." (2 Peter 1:5-7, *Good News Bible*.) "Do your best" means "try your hardest."

The Growing Edge

Look now at the symbol for Christian growth at the front of the chapter. What lessons does it teach concerning Christian growth? List them in your "Log for Journey of Faith." Ask these questions to help you think. What does the symbol say about your character as time passes? Have you grown more at some times than others? Why? What new growth do you need to make?

Are You Ready to Take the Next Step?

It is time now to practice some of the things you have learned in this chapter. We grow by taking the next step we are ready and able to take. You may be ready and able to take one or more of the steps indicated below.

____ Breaking a bad habit.
____ Forgiving someone you have held something against.
____ Planning to attend church camp or conference.
____ Attending a Sunday school class.
____ Going regularly to worship.
____ Beginning daily Bible reading.
____ Forming a friendly relationship with someone of another race.
____ Changing an attitude.
____ Accepting someone you have rejected.
____ Accepting yourself.
____ Accepting your parents without being too critical of them.
____ Attempting to see the viewpoint of your brother or sister.
____ Trying to overcome jealousy.
____ Trying to control your tongue.
____ Doing something good to someone you have not really cared for.
____ Assuming a new responsibility in the home.
____ Beginning to keep your room neat.
____ Beginning to tithe.
____ Beginning to practice daily prayer.
____ Other (*write in*) _____

Jargon for the Journey

Underscore some of the words in this chapter which you do not understand. Look them up in a dictionary.

www.ingramcontent.com/pod-product-compliance
Lightning Source LLC
Chambersburg PA
CBHW080523030426
42337CB00023B/4612